More Historic Rural Churches of Georgia

More HISTORIC RURAL CHURCHES *of* GEORGIA

Sonny Seals

FOREWORD BY ANDREW YOUNG

The University of Georgia Press   Athens

Publication of this book was supported, in part, by the Kenneth Coleman Series in Georgia History and Culture

Published by the University of Georgia Press
Athens, Georgia 30602
www.ugapress.org

Designed by Erin Kirk
Set in Arno Pro
Printed and bound by Friesens
The paper in this book meets the guidelines for permanence and durability of the Committee on Production Guidelines for Book Longevity of the Council on Library Resources.

Most University of Georgia Press titles are available from popular e-book vendors.

Printed in Canada
29 28 27 26 25 C 5 4 3 2 1

EU Authorized Representative
Easy Access System Europe—Mustamäe tee 50, 10621 Tallinn, Estonia, gpsr.requests@easproject.com

Library of Congress Cataloging-in-Publication Data

Names: Seals, Sonny, 1942– author. | Young, Andrew, 1932– writer of foreword. | Erskine, Noel Leo, writer of introduction. | Thompson, Douglas E., writer of introduction.
Title: More historic rural churches of Georgia / Sonny Seals ; foreword by Andrew Young.
Description: Athens : The University of Georgia Press, [2025] | Includes bibliographical references.
Identifiers: LCCN 2024060627 | ISBN 9780820373355 (hardback)
Subjects: LCSH: Church buildings—Georgia. | Historic buildings—Georgia. | Rural churches—Georgia. | Georgia—Church history.
Classification: LCC NA5230.G4 S433 2025 | DDC 726.509758/091734—dc23/eng/20250206
LC record available at https://lccn.loc.gov/2024060627

This book is dedicated to George Hart, my lifelong friend, with a special thanks to Virginia Bolton, Kelly Gomez, and Spencer Roberts. We could not have done this without your passion and your expertise. We have taken a long journey together, with more to come.

Contents

Foreword ANDREW YOUNG

Rural churches were an important factor in my early pastoral career. I grew up in New Orleans in a middle-class neighborhood where my father was a dentist, but as I came of age, I became attracted to the ministry. I graduated from Howard University and decided to attend Hartford Theological Seminary, receiving my divinity degree there in 1955.

My first experience with rural churches had begun in Marion, Alabama, in 1952 where I established a summer Bible school. Marion is located in a remote part of west central Alabama, and it was where I began to experience firsthand the central issues of racial discrimination in the Deep South. This is also where I met my wife, Jean Childs, and we were married there in 1954. Jean was also friends with a schoolmate, Coretta Scott, who married Martin Luther King Jr. in Marion in 1953 at the Scott home.

My first pastoral assignment was from 1955 to 1957 at the Bethany Congregational Church in Thomasville, Georgia. I also pastored Evergreen Congregational Church in the small village of Beachton, Georgia, from 1957 to 1959. Both of these rural churches were historic. Bethany was founded in 1891 and is now on the National Register of Historic Places. Evergreen was founded in 1903 and is on the National Register as well.

Bethany and Evergreen grew out of Allen Normal School, a church-sponsored school founded in the early 1900s. Church-sponsored schools, usually one-room affairs, emerged all over the South in this period as African Americans struggled to create a better life for their children. The churches were the center of the Black communities, and these church-sponsored schools were often the only source of educational opportunity for African American children in the rural areas. As enslaved people, African Americans had not been allowed to learn to read and write, and that struggle for access to education in the Jim Crow South began a long journey that is significant in southern history and the history of our nation.

It was during this period, in 1957, that I first met Dr. King in Talladega, Alabama. We became good friends and after leaving my Evergreen congregation, I joined the Southern Christian Leadership Conference in 1960, moved to Atlanta, and began to work more closely with Dr. King and his colleagues. My first wife, Jean, passed away in 1994. Carolyn McClain and I were married in 1996, and we have accomplished many things together that give us both a great deal of pride.

I have been fortunate to witness many historic and meaningful events as our nation continues to evolve. I am proud to have been a part of that. As I look back, my experience in these rural church assignments was the basis for my understanding of racial inequality in the South and my deeply held conviction to do something about it. It prepared me for the long struggle that was to come. I am proud to be a part of this book that celebrates the rural church histories that are such a big part of that American journey.

Preface

Our first book, *Historic Rural Churches of Georgia*, published in 2016, is now in its fourth printing. After many requests, we are publishing *More Historic Rural Churches of Georgia*, with the help of the University of Georgia Press and our dedicated group of volunteer researchers and photographers. This book will address many aspects of Georgia history that continue to emerge in our study of old rural churches. When we started this journey, we did not know what we would find, but our goal was to somehow raise awareness of these historic treasures and the under-told stories they represent. In the beginning, we outlined four criteria for churches to be included: (1) the congregation must have been formed prior to 1900; (2) the present structure must be at least one hundred years old, with a certain amount of remaining historical architecture; (3) the church must be in a rural location, defined as the countryside or a village with a population of less than two thousand; and (4) ideally, the church has a graveyard. Those are still our criteria.

Historic rural churches are not just buildings—they have stories to tell. Sometimes that story is in the location and the events that took place there. Sometimes it is in the beauty of the setting and the simple architecture, and often the stories are in the old graveyards. These cemeteries contain the remains of the early pioneers, settlers, and enslaved people who helped build our state and our nation. We have found that even with these strict criteria, there are many churches that qualify for inclusion in our database, stored online at www.hrcga.org and in the Historic Rural Church Archive at Pitts Theology Library at Emory University.

Powelton Methodist in Hancock County marked the beginning of our investigation into Georgia's rural churches and their histories.

This book will present a cross section of some of these treasures, representing Black and white congregations as well as geographic and denominational diversity. Rural church histories give us different perspectives of Georgia life in the eighteenth and nineteenth centuries, which reflect some of the seminal events that determined how our new nation was formed. As the state of Georgia emerged from Creek and Cherokee hunting lands, churches were a priority in these new communities—the center of life. They fulfilled the traditional role of providing spiritual comfort, but they also served as community centers, social hubs, dating services, and, to a great extent, enforcers of law and order. The rural churches continue to tell us where we came from and how we got here.

My personal involvement started back in 2012 when my friend and coauthor of the first book, George Hart, and I began taking frequent day trips in the Georgia backcountry. We both found the combination of beautiful landscapes, old towns, abandoned farmhouses, and occasional roadside historical markers fascinating. On one of these trips, I discovered a gravestone for a William D. Seals (1840–1911) in the Powelton Methodist graveyard in the little ghost town of Powelton, in Hancock County. No one in my family had been interested in our genealogy, so I had no idea of my family history beyond my grandfathers. However, with this meager start, and by using the power of the internet and online sources, I soon learned where I came from and how I got here. It turns out William D. Seals was my great-grandfather.

This began a series of discoveries that revealed not only my personal family history but the history of Powelton and other historic villages all across Georgia that struggled to exist in a world that had seen sweeping changes. Many of these old towns have virtually disappeared, leaving behind only a few buildings, churches, and cemeteries to remind us of days gone by. George and I wondered if anyone else cared about these discoveries, so we started a website and began some social networking. This was the beginning of our organization, Historic Rural Churches of Georgia. Early success then led us to write a book and to produce a PBS documentary series. All of this required a network of passionate and skilled volunteer photographers, as well as some deep research into these rural histories. We are grateful for the contributions of these volunteers and their shared passion for Georgia history.

George and I soon began to realize we were seeing Georgia history in a different way. We were looking at history through the eyes of rural churches. We saw that Georgia's history had developed in an unusual manner, relative to that of the other colonies—especially in the way boundaries were formed and land was settled. When Savannah was founded in 1733, Georgia negotiated some land cessations with the Indigenous people along the Savannah River and the coast. But when Georgia became a state after the Revolutionary War, the westward expansion to acquire all Creek and Cherokee land began. This required a series of treaties to acquire massive amounts of territory, river basin by river basin. The process created much conflict with the tribes, especially with the Creeks. As the state's relentless march to the west continued, the Creeks and Cherokees were slowly squeezed out of traditional hunting lands by both Georgia and Alabama, as illustrated in the 1823 map.

The final step was the passage of the Indian Removal Act, authorizing the president to grant unsettled lands west of the Mississippi in exchange for Indigenous lands within existing state borders. It was signed into

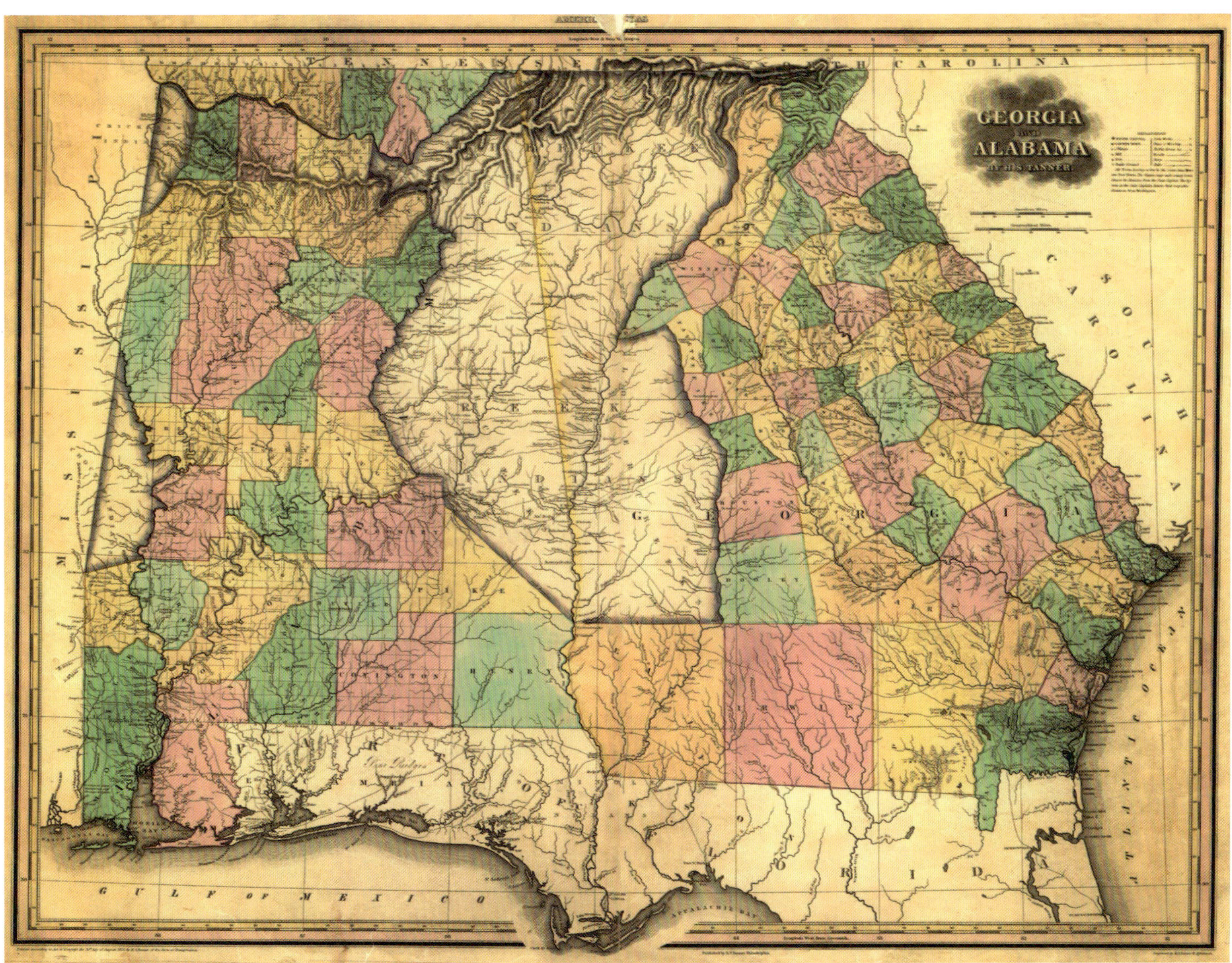

This 1823 map delineates Georgia, Alabama, and Indigenous territories.

law by President Andrew Jackson on May 28, 1830. In 1838, the Cherokees were rounded up and marched to the Oklahoma Territory in what came to be known as the Trail of Tears. Georgia now controlled millions of acres between the Savannah River on the east and the Chattahoochee on the west. Much of this new land was settled by a headright and lottery system, whereby the newly acquired land was divided into small lots and given to white settlers, with preference given to Revolutionary War veterans. The Georgia lottery system conducted eight land lotteries from 1805 to 1833.

At first, Georgia's agricultural wealth was driven by wet rice cultivation in the coastal region. Slavery had been forbidden by the Trustees, who governed Georgia during much of the colonial period, but that changed in 1751 when new legislation permitted slavery for the first time. Affluent planters immigrated from South Carolina and soon began to dominate the coastal economy. Historian Betty Wood, writing in the *New Georgia Encyclopedia*, estimated that in the first twenty-five years after slavery was legalized, "Georgia's enslaved population grew in size from less than 500 to approximately 18,000 people." Slave labor enabled coastal planters to create vast fortunes in the eighteenth and nineteenth centuries, and they built magnificent churches that reflected their status and wealth.

By contrast, the Wiregrass Region of southeast Georgia, just a few miles inland, was far less prosperous, since the area was not suitable for agriculture. In his book *Primitive Baptists of the Wiregrass South*, historian John Crowley notes the region was initially settled by poor Scottish immigrants from South Carolina. It was a hard life in the Wiregrass country, and the churches were reflective of that, particularly those of the Wiregrass Primitive Baptists. In the second half of the eighteenth century the Wiregrass region would begin to generate great wealth in the harvesting of timber, tar, pitch, and turpentine for the global maritime trade. However, these

Midway Congregational was organized in 1752 by early coastal planters—the "rice kings."

exports declined dramatically after 1900, due to the overcutting of the longleaf pine.

Over time, rice faded as an economic source of wealth, but the invention of the cotton gin in Savannah, in 1794, would change America forever. *The American Yawp* notes that in 1800, the United States exported thirty-five million pounds of cotton, representing 7 percent of U.S. exports. By 1860, that number had climbed to 2.3 billion pounds, or more than 60 percent of U.S. exports. Such explosive growth would not have been possible without a corresponding rise in the use of slave labor. Before the advent of the cotton gin, enslavement had been confined to relatively few numbers of wealthy planter families on the East Coast who cultivated tobacco, rice, and long staple cotton. Now the ability to process short staple cotton in the Upcountry resulted in a tremendous surge in demand for enslaved people to work on plantations.

As we researched the church histories, we learned things that were little known but very important in our understanding of cotton and slavery. For instance, according to the website of the Slave Voyages Consortium (slavevoyages.org) approximately twelve million people were enslaved in Africa, put on ships, and sent to the Americas. Due to the horrific conditions and treatment, 1.5 million of them died on the passage. However, of the 10.5 million slaves arriving in the New World, less than 4 percent (four hundred thousand) arrived in North America. The other 96 percent were sent to the Caribbean Islands and to Central and South America to service the sugar trade. Ironically, the United States had outlawed the transatlantic slave trade in 1808. Since slaves could no longer be imported from Africa, this surge in demand for slave labor gave rise to the domestic slave trade.

Planters responded to the increased demand for slave labor by geographically reallocating many of the enslaved people who were already here. *Encyclopedia Virginia* notes that more than a million enslaved people were either sold or forcibly relocated from northern slave states to the South. This reallocation resulted in the separation of

Wayfair Primitive Baptist, in McIntosh County, was organized in 1873.

many families, a tragedy that would be repeated frequently in the first half of the nineteenth century. By the time of the Civil War, there were four million people living in bondage in America, the great majority of them on rural plantations in the South. Many attended white churches, although segregated and supervised. It was not unusual for Black membership to exceed that of whites, sometimes substantially.

Frequently, our research into the histories of the old churches leads to unexpected places. The Prosperity Ridge project, conducted with colleagues from Mercer, Clemson, Emory, and Georgia State Universities, is a case in point. Prosperity Ridge, named for its excellent agricultural properties, is located in northern Greene County. It was settled by migrating Virginia and Carolina planters, who came to dominate the cotton trade in Georgia. Over time, they acquired many slaves for the plantation system that created their wealth. They also established schools and churches. In 1833, the Georgia Baptist Convention established the town of Penfield on Prosperity Ridge with the goal of creating a center of education for future Baptist ministers and the children

Penfield Baptist Church, in Penfield, Greene County, originally served as the Mercer University chapel.

of the planter class. Penfield was the original home of Mercer Institute, later Mercer University, named for famed Baptist minister Jesse Mercer, who is buried in the Penfield cemetery. A magnificent brick church was built in 1845 to serve as the Mercer University chapel. After the war, Mercer was relocated to Macon, where it became one of Georgia's most renowned universities.

Today, Penfield is a ghost town, and the surrounding countryside on Prosperity Ridge is a region of vast forests and sparsely populated farms. There is little to suggest the momentous events that took place here in this remote part of rural Georgia. But Penfield Baptist Church, formerly the Mercer University chapel, still occupies the high ground on the ruins of the old town square.

In the aftermath of the Civil War, newly emancipated slaves, as well as many whites, faced severe economic hardship. Sharecropping was virtually their only means of survival. During this period, churches began to separate along racial lines as African Americans started to form their own rural church communities. However, such religious segregation did not take place spontaneously. Many churches continued to serve Black and white congregants well into the 1870s and beyond. In this postwar environment, most of the emancipated slaves could not read or write. However, they had strong educational aspirations for their children, and many of the African American churches began to sponsor one-room schools that provided the only access to education for many of their children. These schools, with very little county support, sprang up all over Georgia. Very few are still standing.

Over time, as Georgia's economy transitioned from agriculture to industry, the rural population declined along with the rural congregations. In the early 1900s the cotton economy collapsed, resulting in what came to be known as the Great Migration. Southern African Americans began to move to northern and western cities to take factory jobs in order to find a better life. According to the website of the National Archives, approximately six million African Americans left the South between 1910 and 1970. This migration meant some of the rural churches no longer had congregations to sustain them, and they were abandoned. Remnants of these churches, both Black and white, are still out there in the deep woods, but they are rapidly disappearing. For some, weed-covered cemeteries are the only indication they ever existed. We think these abandoned churches are an important part of our history, and we try to research and document all we can, while we can.

We have created a category on our website for these fading structures we call "Almost Gone but Not Forgotten." These haunting relics and their stories are an important part of our Georgia history. These old sanctuaries provided spiritual comfort and social structure for both Black and white congregants, as they struggled to wrest a living from the land in the only way they knew how. Several are featured in this book.

Most of the rural churches have onsite burial grounds. Our research focuses on both the churches and the old graveyards that are attached. The resulting "tales from the crypt" tell us much about the rural pioneers and enslaved people who founded the churches and built these old treasures. The history and genealogy of the African American churches is more difficult to obtain, since much of it was not written down, but we are making progress. We are presently working with colleagues at Emory, Mercer, and Georgia State Universities, as well as the local community, to research and map a large, recently "rediscovered" African American cemetery on Prosperity Ridge, near the town of Penfield.

As previously discussed, approximately four hundred thousand enslaved people (less than 4 percent of the total) were transported from Africa to North America from 1619 to 1808, when the transatlantic African slave trade was banned. In an article in the journal *Slavery & Abolition*, demographic historian J. David Hacker estimates that by 1860, a total of ten million people had been enslaved in North America. He also points out that census records indicate the American slave population was approximately four million in 1860, which means six million people died while enslaved.

That number is sobering and leads us to ask the question: Where are those six million graves? We think

Sandy Grove AME Church School in Warren County was one of the church-affiliated schools that served rural African America children before public education was universally available.

Mount Isaac Baptist in Irwin County is "Almost Gone but Not Forgotten."

Colleagues from Georgia universities and the local community are working to map the African American cemetery at Penfield.

the answer is that the overwhelming majority are buried in unmarked graves throughout the rural South. The Black cemetery at Penfield contains over a thousand unmarked graves, and the initial data suggest many of these are interments of enslaved people who died prior to 1865. The research is ongoing, but we think the Penfield cemetery may provide some insight into this dark period of our history.

Original church minutes often reveal important historical facts. Greene County was formed in 1786, and one of the earliest churches established there was Shiloh Baptist, organized on Town Creek in 1795. The original church is no longer there, but fortunately, some of the minutes (those of 1839–59) survive, as does the original cemetery. Two entries in the minutes are particularly significant. The first is dated April 15, 1855—"Creecy servant to Mrs. M. E. Daniel related an experience and was received [into the membership of the church]." The second is dated January 16, 1859—"Willis Servant to Wm N Williams made application to the church to take a wife as he had been separated from his wife for some time and no expectation of ever being with her any more." We think this means his wife had been sold. The church granted the request, and Willis married Creecy in 1859.

These entries are particularly significant because Willis and Lucrecia (Creecy) were Martin Luther King Jr.'s great-grandparents. After emancipation, they took the surname Williams and raised five children in Greene County. One of them, Adam Daniel "A. D." Williams, was ordained as a Baptist minister in 1880 at Bethabara Church, located close to the village of Scull Shoals. He moved to Atlanta in January 1893 to become pastor of Ebenezer Baptist Church. (For more information about this connection, see the introduction.)

Our Prosperity Ridge research has also revealed President Lyndon Baines Johnson had early Greene County ancestry. It begins with the Battle of Kettle Creek on February 14, 1779, the first major victory for the Patriots in the backcountry of Georgia. Present at that battle were three direct ancestors of the thirty-sixth president of the United States—John Johnson (1764–1828), Nathan Barnett Sr. (1729–1804), and Nathan Barnett Jr. (1758–1822). John was Lyndon's paternal great-great-grandfather and Nathan Sr. was his maternal great-great-great-great-grandfather. After the war, both the Johnsons and the Barnetts were awarded land grants for their service and settled on Prosperity Ridge near Scull Shoals. John's son, Jesse, married Lucy Barnett in 1817, and they eventually migrated to Alabama and then Texas. We find it ironic that exactly two hundred years after John Johnson's birth, two icons of American history with this shared Greene County ancestry, President Lyndon Johnson and the Reverend Martin Luther King Jr., would meet in Washington, D.C., for the signing of the Civil Rights Act of 1964—truly one of our nation's seminal events.

We are pleased that Pitts Theology Library at Emory University recently announced the formation of the Historic Rural Church Archive, which will be the repository of much information regarding rural Georgia churches and their graveyards. This effort will require significant and ongoing collaboration with other libraries, archival repositories, and academic institutions. It will make historical research regarding rural Georgia churches accessible to a much broader audience.

We are honored that Ambassador Andrew Young has written the foreword to this book. He joins his good friend, former president Jimmy Carter, who wrote the foreword for the first book. Both men are giants of our time who spent their lives working tirelessly to make this world a better place. Both had strong feelings about their rural experience and the foundation it provided for their long and fruitful careers. Ambassador Young pastored two rural churches, in Thomas and Grady Counties, in the 1950s. He told us that living and working in the Jim Crow Deep South exerted a profound influence on him and helped lay the foundation for his work with Dr. Martin Luther King Jr. and the civil rights movement. One of the churches he served, Bethany Congregational in Thomas County, is featured in this book.

Finally, we are pleased that two distinguished scholars, Dr. Noel Erskine of Emory University and Dr. Doug Thompson of Mercer University, have cowritten an introduction for this book. Both have deep knowledge of the subject matter, and we feel honored that they share our love of the rural church and its place in our nation's history. Dr. Erskine discusses the Black experience as he traces the movement from Africa, the Caribbean, and South America through the development of the American plantation system. Dr. Thompson continues the discussion of that experience up until the Civil War, with a particular emphasis on his Penfield / Prosperity Ridge research, which is so relevant to this book.

Much of our rural church history has been lost. Gaining access to these early records is difficult, particularly so with regard to the African American churches, since many of those records were not written down. As rural populations have declined, so have the church congregations supporting them, and the knowledge remaining congregants hold is fast disappearing. A case in point is the beautiful church on this book's jacket—Rehobeth CME in Lamar County. Rehobeth is typical of many abandoned sanctuaries you see on the Georgia backroads that were once the center of rural life in a time of agricultural dominance that no longer exists. This book honors that legacy.

Old rural churches continue to inform our view of Georgia history and that of our nation. We believe that in order to understand America's journey from its beginning to the present, we must understand southern history, and that history is predominantly rural. It is white, it is Black, and much of it is dark—but it is ours. We need to own it and learn from it. Rural church history tells us where we came from and how we got here. It tells us who we are. We hope you enjoy this book—the stories continue.

SONNY SEALS

Introduction NOEL LEO ERSKINE AND DOUGLAS E. THOMPSON

The histories of rural churches and their congregations do not tell themselves. From the simple, wooden box constructions of the Primitive Baptists in the Wiregrass to stunning, unique creations such as Antioch Baptist Church, these physical structures and spaces serve as fixed points in the shifting environment of rural Georgia. Their walls echo with the voices of generations long passed. Their church minutes record the religious, social, and economic lives of community members. For many nineteenth-century Black congregants in particular, church buildings and church records may offer the only documentation of their lives outside of slave schedules, bills of sale, or estate appraisals. But hidden in the pages of church activities are glimpses of love, dedication, belief, worship, and humanity. Uncovering and learning from these remnants of the past requires dedicated time, effort, and collaboration between many partners. The following pages explore the depths of the past made visible through the lens of rural churches and examine the lives of people whose stories demonstrate the value of religion and churches in understanding the history of rural Georgia.

FROM AFRICA TO THE NEW WORLD PLANTATION

In his important book, The Negro Church in America, historian E. Franklin Frazier advanced the thesis that the plantation economy eviscerated the last vestiges of African life and customs among oppressed people trapped on plantations in the New World. According to Frazier, plantation life destroyed social cohesion and African understandings of work as a cooperative undertaking. Slavery was more than an economic institution; it was also a political force designed to produce a disciplined and dependent slave. For Frazier, the historical record was not merely broken but lost. This meant that Africans in the New World encountered the plantation as the primary means and method of European colonization. Theories of survival and decolonization were not found in their myths, stories, and the memory of Africa, but in accommodation and adaptation to their new environment with the master's book, the Bible, being the source of social organization and survival in a strange land and "a long ways from home." One goal of plantation slavery was to be a constant reminder to enslaved persons of their place at the bottom of society and the need to stay in their place if they were to survive.

Frazier was insistent that Africans were a people without a heritage and that the way forward for them was with tools provided by the master. Could Africans marooned in the Americas free themselves with these tools? Regarding religion, the main tool was the Bible. Frazier placed in perspective the precarity of life in the New World for Africans "stolen from the homeland": "The enslavement of the Negro not only destroyed the traditional African system of kinship and other forms of organized social life, but it made insecure and precarious the most elementary form of social life which tended to sprout anew, so to speak, on American soil—the family. There was, of course, no legal marriage and the relation of the husband and father to his wife and children was a temporary relationship dependent upon the will of white masters and the exigencies of the plantation regime."[1]

Church historian Gayraud Wilmore in *Black Religion and Black Radicalism* agreed with Frazier that the Christian scriptures were shared with enslaved persons. However, he also noted Africa's children did not present themselves as a tabula rasa but applied Christianity in the context of their suffering and quest for freedom. The freedom of oppressed Black people to apply missionary teaching to their existential needs, Wilmore wrote, advanced "important discontinuities between the Christian religion among white Americans and that same religion as it is practiced in the segregated Black communities of the United States and the West Indies. . . . It is certain that by the beginning of the eighteenth century there were a few Black church members in all the colonies—most of them worshipping in the same churches with their masters, or if freedmen, with their white neighbors—albeit under conditions of segregation."[2]

Despite his insistence that slavery had wiped out all traces of African heritage, E. Franklin Frazier was aware of sources that claimed otherwise, especially in the Sea Islands along the coast of Georgia and South Carolina, where they were preserved in oral history through the dialect known as Gullah. He also cited W. E. B. Du Bois, who had pointed out that social cohesion among enslaved persons was not totally destroyed. "The Negro Church," Frazier wrote, quoting Du Bois, "was 'the only social institution among Negroes which started in the African forest and survived slavery,' and that 'under the leadership of the priest and medicine man' the church preserved the remnants of African tribal life."[3]

Du Bois was clear that the marks of the Black church were the preacher, the music, and the frenzy and that the Black church was not at first a Christian church but an African one. Moreover, he said, it took about two centuries for African religious practices to become Christian. More recent scholars of the Black experience in America point out that prior to the 1770s, Black people in America were not exposed to much Christian teaching or preaching. It was not until the nineteenth-century awakenings that Black people in any meaningful numbers were able to attend religious services with regularity, under the proviso from the missionary that conversion or baptism would not mean freedom or equality with white persons. With Du Bois we may agree that religious practices and beliefs brought over from Africa did not constitute a formal unified religion, yet Africa's children were able to adapt their religious beliefs to the strange and alien world that confronted them on plantations, "a long ways from home."

Lawrence Levine in *Black Culture and Black Consciousness* articulated early words from the African church as the enslaved community related the Bible to their African context:

> The Bible, in fact, could be used to prove the efficacy of sacred folk beliefs. "Does I believe in spirits?" Charles Hayes [an enslaved person] asked. "Sho I does. When Christ walked on the water, de Apostles was skeered he was a spirit, but Jesus told dem dat he warn't no spirit, dat he was as 'live as dey was. . . . He tol' 'em dat spirits couln't be teched, dat dey jus' melted when you try to. So, Mistis, Jesus musta meant dat dere was sich a thing as spirits." Thomas Smith of Georgia made the same point more forcefully when he insisted that the magic power used by Moses to turn his rod into a snake before Pharaoh still exists among Negroes. "Dat happen in Africa duh Bible say. Ain dat show dat Africa wuz a lan uh magic powuh since duh beginnin uh histry? Well den, duh descendants ub Africans hab duh same gif tuh do unnatchul ting."[4]

This blending of African ways of thinking with the Christian narrative, coupled with an attempt to make it relevant to the new situation that confronted Africa's children in the New World, gets at what Du Bois had in mind when he asserted that the preacher / medicine man was the main link between Africa and plantation life. According to Du Bois, the preacher / medicine man "early appeared on the plantation and found his function as the healer of the sick, the interpreter of the Unknown, the comforter of the sorrowing, the supernatural avenger of wrong, the one who rudely but picturesquely expressed the longing, disappointment, and resentment of a stolen and oppressed people."[5]

On most plantations the only religion that was allowed by masters was Christianity. Africa's children found ways of practicing what we may term a hermeneutic of return as they were ingenious in relating their ancestors and African customs to the Christian God introduced to them by missionaries.

African priests during New World slavery served on plantations by helping Africa's children navigate life. They instilled in the oppressed community the confidence that "Massa" did not have all the power, or the last word in relation to people's lives. The African priest would mediate between the living and the dead and serve as a symbol of hope. The priest was able to help fellow Africans discover Africa in the Americas, through storytelling, Negro spirituals, and notions of spirit power, which would facilitate their return to Africa when they died. The priest / medicine man could divine the present because he lived on the boundary, so to speak, between life and death. Through songs of hope and prayers of liberation, Africa's children would dream of a new day "when the troubles of this world would be over" and their descendants would witness the inbreak of liberation. Africa's children would sing:

> I don't know how to get on the other side,
> One mo' ribber to cross,
> Oh, you got Jesus, hold him fast,
> One mo' ribber to cross,
> Oh, better love was nebber told,
> One mo' ribber to cross.[6]

For the first fifteen years of the Georgia colony's existence, slavery was outlawed, and therefore few of Africa's children worked the fields. But after the 1751 shift to embrace the use of enslaved labor, persons in bondage resided primarily along the coastal plain of the province. Georgia's Sea Islands in particular provided a safe haven for the melding of religious identities.

THE RISE OF INDEPENDENT BLACK CHURCHES

The evangelical revival of the 1740s known as the Great Awakening seemed to bring about a change of heart among white church leaders, prompting them—possibly for the first time—to look favorably on the idea of independent Black churches and preachers. It is important to note that these church leaders were not calling for freedom and liberation of enslaved persons; rather, their emphasis and advocacy were for spiritual salvation—the so-called saving of the soul—while the body remained in bondage. Virginia Baptist John Leland framed the issue this way:

> The poor slaves, under all their hardships, discover as great an inclination for religion as the freeborn do, when they engage in the service of God, they spare no pains. It is nothing strange for them to walk twenty miles on Sunday morning to meeting and back again at night. . . . They seem in general to put more confidence in their own colour, then [*sic*] they do in whites; when they attempt to preach, they seldom fail of being very zealous; their language is broken, but they understand each other, and the whites may gain their ideas. A few of them have undertaken to administer baptism, but it generally ends in confusion; they commonly are more noisy in time of preaching than whites.[7]

During the Great Awakening many slavers were persuaded by missionaries to allow their enslaved people to attend revival services. James Melvin Washington informs us that several enslaved persons, including George Liele, would attend religious worship not for doctrinal purposes but because their needs were existential, and the worship experience, often in the open air, provided a measure of freedom for community with each other. Sermons of divine justice gave them confidence in a just God who would punish all persons, including the master. According to Washington, "They believed that spiritual bondage was a greater affliction than material bondage, and that freedom from one might lead to freedom of the other. They knew that their churches were chattel arrangements. But they stubbornly trusted in the promises of the Bible that God is a liberator."[8]

One illuminating example is the religious life of George Liele, the first African American baptized and licensed to preach in a white church, Big Buckhead Baptist Church in Georgia. Liele's master, Henry Sharp, was a deacon at the church and the brother-in-law of pastor Matthew Moore.[9]

In an article published in 1943, John Palmer Gates documented Liele's ministry at his home church in rural Georgia:

> As to his religious life Liele relates, "I always had a natural fear of God from my youth" which had the effect of "barring me from many sins and bad company." In about the year 1773, while listening one sabbath afternoon to Matthew Moore, pastor of the Kiokee church, he became convinced that he was "not in the way to heaven, but in the way to hell." . . . He was baptized by Moore and admitted into fellowship of the church. It was not long until it became evident that Liele was "possessed of ministerial gifts" and was permitted by his master to "instruct" the colored people on the estate. The privilege was later extended to include other plantations along the Savannah River. His method at first, according to Rippon, was to read hymns to his fellow slaves, encouraging them to sing and then to explain the "most striking parts to them." Soon he was given the opportunity to preach for the congregation at Kiokee whereupon they granted him a license to preach as a probationer. . . . He was finally ordained, May 20 1775.[10]

Liele's freedom to boat along the Savannah River took him to Silver Bluff, South Carolina, where he functioned as one of the leaders of the Silver Bluff Baptist Church.

While serving as a missionary in Jamaica, Liele wrote to John Rippon of *The Baptist Annual Register* about his conversion in Georgia:

"I saw my condemnation in my own heart, and found no way wherein I could escape the damnation of hell, only through the merits of my dying Lord and Savior Jesus Christ; which caused me to make intercession with Christ, for the salvation of my poor immortal soul; and I full well recollect, I requested of my Lord and Master to give me a work, I did not care how mean it was, only to see how well I could do it."[11]

Liele stated that he was overwhelmed with feelings of damnation and felt sentenced to spend eternity in hell. However, he found an answer to these feelings of unworthiness—solidarity with the suffering and dying Christ, who would intercede on his behalf and save his "poor immortal soul." There emerged in Liele's testimony a special relationship between himself and Jesus—a relationship that transcended the one between Liele and his earthly master. As divine lord and master, Jesus not only offered deliverance from condemnation and damnation in hell but also provided worthwhile work for his followers. Liele stated that he did not care how menial this work might be; all he asked for was strength to do the work to the best of his ability. This new relationship with Jesus opened the door to possibilities of love and fellowship with fellow enslaved persons and an understanding of Jesus that gave Liele the right to claim equality in the presence of God with all persons, including his earthly master.

Liele believed that if he were faithful in teaching the word of Christ through hymns and Bible study, there would be a breakthrough, in God's time, from the terror of New World slavery. Perhaps this confidence in the providence of God came from his history as a Particular Baptist who believed that God in God's own time would make all things new.

In *Theology in America: Christian Thought from the Age of the Puritans to the Civil War*, E. Brooks Holifield suggests that Calvinist theology in the Black community had its deepest roots in the Baptist Church, leading to belief in an "Afro-Baptist Sacred Cosmos" that drew on both African and Christian worldviews. African preachers in both the eighteenth and nineteenth centuries combined African and Christian ways of viewing the world in their approach to survival and liberation as they sought to dismantle the house of bondage. Holifield cites Liele's witness to what was perhaps the kernel of his Calvinistic faith: "I agree to election, redemption, the fall of Adam, regeneration, and perseverance, knowing that the promise is that all who endure, in grace, faith and good works to the end, shall be saved."[12]

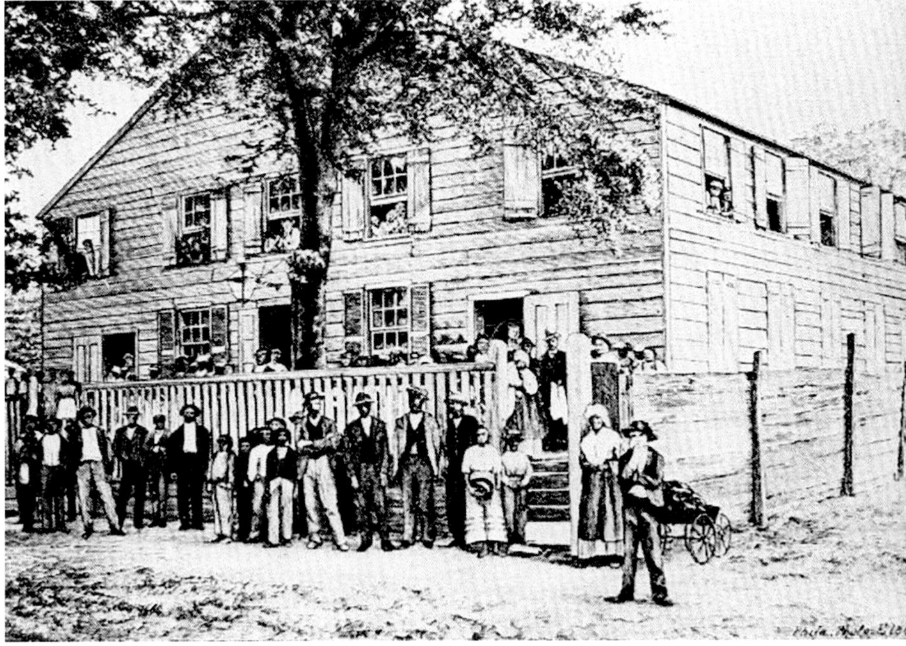

Silver Bluff Baptist, organized in 1774–76, was the first independent Black church in the United States.

In this short synopsis of his theological position, Liele turned the spotlight on theological claims gleaned from Big Buckhead Baptist Church. His short description of church teaching encompassed both the sin of human beings as they turned away from God and against each other and the divine answer of redemption and regeneration, made possible through the suffering and dying Christ.[13]

A Christological point of departure stood at the core of Liele's theology, as Christ—the master who was above all masters—reversed the damnation and bondage that Adam's children deserved and, in their place, guaranteed salvation at the end of life's journey. In his covenant and synopses of sermons, Liele highlighted Christ, who offered deliverance from sin as signified by his own suffering and dying, combined with eternal life and felicity with himself for all who endured to the end. The vision of the end—being with Christ—was reserved for all who were faithful as they discovered that God would keep God's promise to Adam's children.

Despite the violence of plantation life, Liele found hope in contemplating the next life. He gestured in the direction of St. Paul's words in 1 Corinthians 15:22, "For as in Adam all die, so also in Christ shall all be made alive" (Revised Standard Version). In Liele's theological worldview was an eschatological horizon that provided energy for the journey from slavery to liberation for all who continued to the end, summed up in a call to duty and faithfulness: "knowing that the promise is that all who endure, in grace, faith and good works to the end, shall be saved."[14]

It should be noted that George Liele, Henry Sharp, and pastor Matthew Moore gave allegiance to the British flag rather than siding with the revolutionary forces. When the British occupied Savannah in 1778, members of the Silver Bluff Church fled to that city to be under the protection of the British. Historian Carter G. Woodson wagered that among them were David George and Jesse Peters, who served as leaders of the congregation at Silver Bluff. However, among the British in Savannah they would not have had much influence to secure a permit to serve the congregation as pastors. Because of his close relationship with Moses Kirkland, the head of the British forces in Savannah, it was advantageous for Liele to serve as pastor of a congregation in the war-torn city, since he would need a license to preach. Woodson pointed out, "Out of this effort of George Liele developed what Dr. Brooks considers the first Negro Baptist Church in the city of Savannah, which flourished during the British occupation from 1779 to the year 1782.[15] The oldest Negro Baptist Church in this country, however, is that of the Silver Bluff Church which, in another meeting place and under a new name, became established at Augusta, having existed from the year 1773 to 1793 before the time of Andrew Bryan's organizing efforts in Savannah."[16]

Under the leadership of pastor Matthew Moore and deacon Henry Sharp, Big Buckhead Baptist Church in Jenkins County provided space for the ministry of George Liele.

One of the last acts George Liele performed prior to his departure from Savannah to Jamaica was to baptize Andrew Bryan, who would succeed him as pastor of First African Baptist Church of Savannah. Bryan and the membership of this church were in for a long season of persecution from the citizens of Savannah, who did not forget that the church leaders supported the British during the war. When the British left Savannah in 1782, Liele and his pastor at Big Buckhead Baptist Church accompanied them.[17] The congregation at Big Buckhead Baptist Church dwindled following the revolution but possibly reemerged in Jamaica through the Ethiopian Baptist Church, which Liele established a couple of years after his arrival in that country. Liele devoted the remainder of his life to the planting of Baptist churches in Jamaica.

BLACK CONGREGATIONS FROM SLAVERY TO EMANCIPATION

From the American Revolution until the end of the War of 1812, Georgia had limited growth west except along river routes, most notably the Savannah River near Augusta. That initial movement and the creation of Columbia County brought more settlers into the areas that would become Wilkes, Greene, and Oglethorpe Counties. While the cotton gin had made the processing of cotton bolls easier and the growing of short staple upland cotton more financially lucrative, Native peoples—mostly Cherokee and Muscogee Creek—controlled much of the interior of Georgia. But as land opened, first through treaties and then through removal, demand for enslaved labor grew exponentially. By the 1830s, much of the land from the Ocmulgee River eastward had been settled. Across the swath of land, later known as the Black Belt for its rich topsoil, that stretched from Richmond, Virginia, down through Macon, Georgia, and over to East Texas, white planters led the charge to secure more land and build a political and religious world that affirmed their understanding of the divine order of things.

Meanwhile, the Great Awakening in the mid-Atlantic and New England colonies around the middle of the eighteenth century helped give rise to the idea of revivals as ongoing movements, and the second eruption of them involved the expanding American frontier and the American South. Though the southern frontier saw growth in Protestant groups such as Baptists, Methodists, and Presbyterians, the expansion of religious groups also mirrored the growth of the domestic slave trade.

Those who built churches such as Shiloh Baptist or Penfield Baptist saw themselves as purveyors of order and rational thought. They watched carefully over their flocks to make sure that people who broke their rules understood the gravity of their behavior, and they extended the "hand of fellowship" to a brother or sister who had strayed only after a public confession of wrong to the community.

These white Christian slavers worried more about the spiritual welfare of their enslaved people than many eighteenth-century slavers had, in part because they could see the controlling nature of their version of religion. But others in their midst heard the gospel message of salvation to the captives and recognized themselves in the arc of divine history. As in earlier encounters with European forms of Christianity, Africa's children shaped the message to reflect their own understanding of the divine in their lives. Enslaved preachers of the nineteenth century embraced the continuity of God's plan for creation just as white Protestants did, but with a different emphasis. These preachers noted that God had sided with the enslaved in Egypt, and that the Godhead in the form of Jesus was born of lowly status. If the enslavers believed that God ordered the world in their images, the enslaved heard the gospel call to personal liberation and corporate freedom. The former, interested in order, resisted notions of equality, even in the Holy Spirit, because God could not create the world and heaven differently. The latter knew that the God of Israel and Jesus always inverted the order created by those on high.

Whether in field hollers, plantation rhythms, or worship houses with white Protestants, enslaved and freed people in the American South formed a Christian identity that was theirs, rather than following the dictates of white Christians who debated whether to even let them worship. Even before emancipation—-which occurred more through the success of Union troops in Georgia in 1864 than through the proclamation in 1863—Black Protestants had developed organizational and leadership skills that they used to create the first institutional structures of freedom. Black Christian congregations had already been in existence for much of the nineteenth century, even if in limited ways.

GREENE COUNTY, KING COTTON, AND RELIGION

In July 1842, the membership at Penfield Baptist Church, barely three years old, discussed "the propriety of admitting Blacks to membership with us." In usual Baptist fashion, a committee formed to survey white residents about the issue. The verdict, according to the congregation's discussion as reported in the church minutes, was no. More than three years passed before an enslaved person was welcomed with the "right hand of fellowship," a Baptist euphemism regarding membership. In the minutes book, however, the first mention of a Black member is in an entry regarding "Letters of dismission" for John Harris, his sister Jane Harris, "and also to a colored sister, Patsy."[18] Patsy's membership record is not included in the minutes, which must reflect an oversight by the church clerk, since she had to be a member in good standing to receive one of these letters.

Penfield formed as a town in 1837 to meet the needs of the growing Georgia Baptist school Mercer University. Lots laid out from the Georgia Baptist Convention's (GBC) purchase of almost 1,000 acres of uncultivated land show the design of the town, with Mercer University as its center. Mercer had formed in 1833 as an "institute" for students to prepare for university-level work. By 1837, the GBC decided to use the early success of the institute to build the first Baptist university in Georgia, so their sons did not have to go to Columbian University (later George Washington University) in Washington, D.C., or other northern universities.

The land, however, served as an equal attraction to Georgia planters, including the first president of Mercer, Billington M. Sanders. Trained at both Franklin College (now the University of Georgia) and South Carolina College (now the University of South Carolina), Sanders briefly led an academy before adopting the planter's life of his upbringing. Sanders and his older sister and younger brother were minors when their parents died, thus inheriting their father's planter wealth, including an equal division of the twenty-one enslaved humans their father had owned. When Billington graduated from South Carolina College at the age of eighteen in 1809, he held as property seven of those people and held in trust the seven willed to his brother. Within a decade, Sanders prospered as a planter. Recognized for his talents, he served on a grand jury, was elected as an inferior court justice, and legislated as a representative for one term in the Georgia statehouse. By 1830, he had amassed a 600-acre plantation in Columbia County and a newly built home.

Billington's decision to leave the comfort of a planter's life in Columbia County to settle on the Georgia frontier in Greene County led later biographers to ignore the planter to focus on the minister. Indian removal, begun in earnest in 1830, had made the journey easier and the risk lighter to pack up a family and a few enslaved people to move to Greene County. He would not sell the Columbia County plantation for another five years, when he also moved the larger number of his enslaved people to work his plantation in Penfield. Left out of the white Protestant telling of the frontier story was the fact that the land was ripe for planting, particularly for the emerging upland cotton seed that centered American planters in the global cotton markets. The growing value of enslaved property was about to make all the men who created Penfield extraordinarily wealthy.[19]

The Penfield Baptist Church minutes book is a window into white Christians' growing sense of responsibility for their human property's spiritual well-being. Like many records of various white congregations across the nineteenth-century American South, these minutes reveal details of congregational life—rules of decorum and how congregations dealt with violators—and the ways that these people approached the monumental shifts in American Christianity, particularly around the Bible and property rights. The entry about allowing enslaved persons membership in the church is one such example.

By the mid-1840s, the number of enslaved people in Penfield had climbed to over 100; eight years later, it was above 250. By comparison, if the students at Mercer and a female academy in Penfield were left out, white Penfield citizens numbered under fifty in the early to mid-1840s. The fact that the mother church, Shiloh Baptist, had admitted Black members prior to the 1840s suggests that not all white Georgia Baptists were reluctant to include their human property in membership. But Penfield's minutes book indicates that the congregation struggled to reach a clear consensus. By June 1845, however, the church conference voted to create a committee "to suggest a plan for the religious instruction of our black

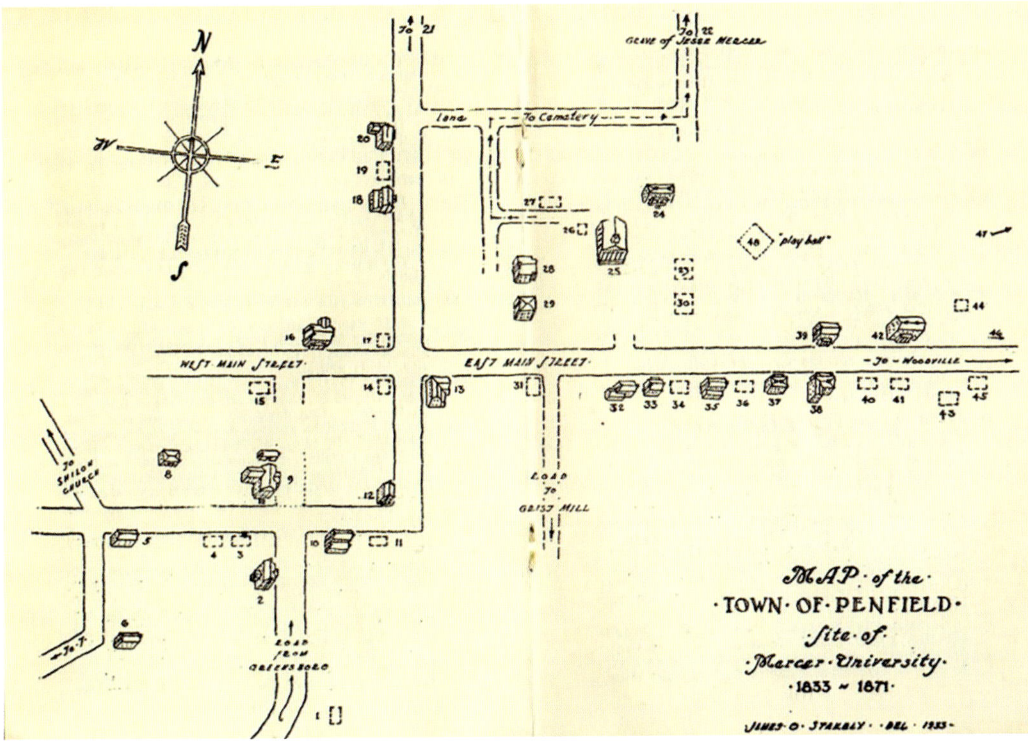

The town of Penfield was founded in 1837.

population." Six months later, the conference "voted, That the Pastor and three lay brethren be appointed to make arrangements for religious instruction to the blacks, and report at next conference meeting."[20] The minutes book leaves out all mention of the agency in religious instruction that the Black people of Penfield exercised. Were the Black members reminding their white brothers in Christ that they too had need for religious instruction? Since we know that independent Black congregations, even under the supervision of white overseers, had developed in Georgia as early as the late colonial period, was there pressure to create an independent Black congregation in Penfield? Or as had been the case for much of the previous century, were the enslaved people in Penfield already providing religious life for their own outside the purview of white Baptists in Penfield? Regardless of the reason, by the mid-1850s, there was an independent Black Baptist congregation in Penfield.

One mile south of the now-abandoned Penfield, on the road to Greensboro, is Sanders Chapel Baptist Church. A single-story concrete block building, painted white, it sits just off Penfield Road. Behind the building, a small cemetery that comes near the back of the building has been overgrown by the reforesting process that covers much of this part of Greene County. The land on which the building and cemetery sit was part of Billington M. Sanders's large landholdings. Sanders Chapel bears the name of its benefactor. Less than one mile south stands Boswell Baptist Church, named for another of the prominent white families in the region. Five miles northwest lies the reforested cemetery of a significant congregation, Bethabara Baptist Church (signage on the Penfield Road says Bethel Bara). All three congregations had some connection to Penfield.

The Reverend Adam Daniel "A. D." Williams, born enslaved in Penfield, had been licensed and ordained at Bethabara before migrating to Atlanta in the 1890s. There he founded Ebenezer Baptist Church, which would rise in fame first through Williams and his son-in-law, the Reverend Martin Luther King Sr., and then from 1960 to 1968 through the work of his grandson, Martin Luther King Jr., and his organization for civil rights, the Southern Christian Leadership Conference (SCLC). Bethabara Baptist Church has disappeared except for a large stepping stone and the reforested cemetery nearby. A timber company owns the property where the church used to sit.

A. D. Williams's migration from Greene County to Atlanta, and his rise as a significant political force for Black citizens of his community there, provides a lens to see how Black communities form around churches but also why mobility, a gift in many ways, served as a death knell for congregations like Bethabara as spaces became defined as rural in the twentieth century. While Bethabara was relatively close to a thriving Black community near Scull Shoals (sometimes spelled Skull Shoals) in the late 1800s, it fell victim to the loss of industry as the Scull Shoals Factory failed due to natural disaster and was taken apart and removed to enlarge the Athens Foundry or sold as scrap metal in 1890.[21]

Sanders Chapel Baptist Church, however, is an example of a community that retained its identity in rural Georgia. As C. Eric Lincoln and Lawrence H. Mamiya have shown, if rural Black congregations remained cohesive into the middle of the twentieth century, they often continue to serve their members into the present, even without pastors present all week because of their itinerant status. Their lay leaders carry the load, and thus the churches often remain active, even with small numbers.[22] Location, however, also plays a significant role in rural congregations' existence. Sanders Chapel and Boswell Chapel sit on the road that connects Penfield to the county seat, Greensboro.

The period from emancipation until 1900 created both an optimism and a harsh reality for African American institutions in Georgia. Black congregations were quickly established across the state, in part because Baptists and Methodists had found ways to encourage Black membership during the prewar era, often in separate congregations like those seen at Penfield. Another factor was that church property owned by white planters before emancipation transferred to self-sufficient Black congregations following the war. Once those bodies within Baptist life found their footing, they started building new congregations, outside of white citizens' purview, in areas their members had settled.

Penfield Baptist Church created an independent Black congregation, under white supervision, in the 1850s. One of the congregations to grow out of that church was Sanders Chapel. Shiloh Baptist Church does not appear to have allowed its members to congregate independently, but in the aftermath of emancipation, both Boswell Chapel and Bethabara congregated and then built themselves into churches. Their membership included people from Shiloh and Penfield, as well as newly freed people on the Thomas Poullain plantation at Scull Shoals.

In Methodist life, the process looked different as the episcopal structure places congregations under the care of a bishop. The influx of African Methodist Episcopal (AME) and AME Zion preachers / missionaries to Georgia created independent congregations within independent Black denominations. But there were Black Methodists in the American South who established their independence from both white and northern-affiliated Black Methodists. The denomination long known as the Colored Methodist Episcopal Church altered its organizational name in the mid-twentieth century to the Christian Methodist Episcopal Church, while keeping its acronym (CME). In the postwar years, a small number of Black Methodists remained in connection with the white Methodist Episcopal Church, South.

Presbyterians had often had a tough time establishing Black congregations but achieved limited success with missionary outreach to Black middle-class urbanites. A similar issue existed for the Protestant Episcopal and Roman Catholic Churches in Georgia. Congregations grew mostly in urban spaces, the result of missionary activity in the twentieth century. Many of the Black churches in this volume are Baptist and Methodist due to the formation of independent congregations during the antebellum era. Their missionary impulse meant they actively built congregations wherever their members moved across the landscape.

Before emancipation, the worship practices of Black congregations were often prescribed and monitored by white overseers. For example, at the January 1846 meeting of the Penfield Church in conference, the clerk noted, "Your committee are informed, that the House, formerly occupied by Bro. (Pleasant) Chandler has been given to the blacks for a place of religious meetings." Preaching would be carried out by white men in the town twice per month, but the clerk indicated that the Black members of Penfield could attend Shiloh Baptist Church the other two Sundays of each month. The church conference stated that enslaved members could also hold evening prayer meetings every Sunday "to be chiefly conducted by the blacks themselves." Four prominent white men in Penfield were assigned to "attend" these prayer meetings and "procure the attendance of two other white persons."[23]

Under Georgia law at the time, any group of Black persons numbering three or more had to be under the supervision of a white overseer. But in these spaces, Black members appeared to have some say over their affairs. In an entry for October 14, 1849, Lemuel Greene, a white planter in Penfield, noted that "the colored church met in conference, Bro. Lipford presided." The church meeting passed a resolution "'That we will in future have an annual missionary sermon preached and take a collection to be appropriated to the African Mission.'"[24] With this limited entry in the minutes, it is hard to know whether the African mission originated with the white congregation or emerged from the Black congregation's role of missionary activity in Africa and desire to contribute to the work there. "Bro. Lipford" seems to be Henry F. Lipford, who had joined the Penfield congregation in the spring of 1849. In an entry for February 7, 1852, the clerk,

S. P. Sanford, indicated that the Black congregation had chosen a preacher among themselves for one Sunday per month. "[The white congregation] voted," he wrote, "that the Church approve of the Colored branch of this church calling Boson a colored brother to supply them with preaching one Sabbath in each month."[25] Throughout the 1850s and early 1860s the recording process and approval of the Black congregation's business remained under the watchful eye of the white members of Penfield Baptist Church, but after the Civil War the running of the Black congregation shifted to Black members themselves.

As with Silver Bluff Baptist Church in South Carolina and First African Baptist Church in Savannah, Sanders Chapel Baptist Church began the process of removing white oversight of their worship experiences following emancipation. Freedom within the context of worship was not new to them, but the legal structure around overseers changed. White members of Penfield Baptist Church, like white Christians across the American South, assumed that their paternalistic attitudes toward their Black brothers and sisters in Christ would continue to be welcomed. That assumption, however, proved to be wrong. Unaware, or simply too wrapped up in notions of supremacy to understand, white members of Penfield Baptist Church had spent almost two decades allowing their enslaved members to develop skills of institution building by having a separate congregational life. When political emancipation came, congregational emancipation followed. Church records are silent about how and when the two congregations formally parted ways. In Baptist parlance, Penfield Baptist Church should have issued letters of dismission to their Black members to join another Baptist congregation. There is no such entry in the minutes—a striking omission for a congregation so attached to the rules of church membership. It is a sign that when emancipation came, Black members asserted their freedom and continued to worship and minister in their own congregation without concern about what white members thought or did.

Adam Daniel "A. D." Williams may be the most famous son of the congregation known as Bethabara Baptist Church. Bethabara formed under the leadership of the Reverend Parker Poullain, who had been enslaved on Dr. Thomas Poullain's plantation located near the falls on the Oconee River, known as Scull Shoals. Born to Willis and Lucrecia Williams in the 1860s, A. D. entered the world enslaved and spent his earliest years on the Daniel plantation with his mother, Creecy. Both of his parents were listed in the Shiloh Baptist Church minutes book, so A. D. would have been part of that congregation's life until emancipation.[26] At the time of the 1870 U.S. census, Willis and Creecy lived with their five children on William N. Williams's plantation in Penfield. Listed separately from the white Williamses with their occupation given as farmers, they were part of the sustained agricultural life of the cotton plantation system after the American Civil War. Willis was also an itinerant preacher.[27]

Willis died prior to 1874, and little is known about the lives of Creecy or her children until part of the family reappears in an anomalous entry in the 1880 U.S. census in the house of Barney Maxey in Scull Shoals. Adam and Eve Williams are listed with the correct ages but are identified as "W" (white). Between their names is a Creecy (in every other case this name and its variations stand in for Lucrecia), who was listed as four years old and "W." Given that the enumerator listed them as "Servant" but in the household, the "racial" designation is an error. The entry for Creecy is probably also inaccurate, since there was no child in the Williams family with that name. If the enumerator could misidentify the "racial" status, he could have easily forgotten to write the *0* after the *4*. In 1880, Lucretia would have been forty.[28]

We know from biographical sketches that A. D. Williams was in Scull Shoals by 1880. Less well known is that shortly before Willis's death, William N. Williams had his 565 acres of land identified in a lawsuit brought by the administrator of John E. McCarter's estate and announced as part of a sheriff's sale on January 1, 1874.[29]

Even though Willis showed enough property value to appear in the tax digest in the early 1870s (with property valued at $200), he did not own land. In emancipation, he and his family existed in the precarity of both agricultural life and the broader crop-lien systems that made him and them subject to the land.[30]

A. D. Williams moved to the Scull Shoals area to work in the burgeoning industry along the Oconee River. The 1880 census suggests he worked land alongside Maxey because the latter held the designation "farmer." Family lore, however, also has A. D. working at a sawmill in Scull Shoals where he lost part of one thumb.[31] Within three miles of the industry that grew up alongside the river, African Americans had carved out of the land a Baptist congregation called Bethabara, free from the strictures of antebellum life. The Reverend Parker Poullain led the flock. The congregation would have been a mix of day laborers from the fields and factories in and around the north Greene County area. Now hidden among reforested land, Bethabara Baptist Church's cemetery holds markers that date from the early twentieth century and many older undated markers. Community knowledge of this space existed long after the community had begun to leave.

In 1890, the factories began to fade from Scull Shoals, and the disastrous effects of overplanting cotton without sufficient natural fertilizers to replenish the soil meant that work and life in the region were precarious. Licensed and ordained to preach in Bethabara Baptist Church, A. D. Williams served mostly as an itinerant preacher, like his father. Few rural ministers had the same fortune as their white planter predecessors who made money off their plantations. But the Williams family had already shown a willingness to move from the plantation to Scull Shoals. This form of mobility, circumscribed by factors often beyond their control, became part of Black religious experience in rural spaces. We think of the Great Migration that happened some forty years later, but A. D. Williams and his family had been among the first in a trickle of movement, initially within the same geographic location and then beyond that location—Penfield to Scull Shoals and later to Atlanta.

A. D. Williams's departure from Greene County did not bring an end to Bethabara Baptist Church, but it did serve as a notice for rural congregations born in spaces that were not overly populated. By the late 1890s he would move to Atlanta, serving as an itinerant preacher until 1899 when he and his wife, Jennie Parks Williams, committed to the small congregation at Ebenezer Baptist Church. He quickly grew the congregation to more than four hundred members and helped establish a model for urban Black congregations, growing in part from the influx of other people leaving rural spaces like northern Greene County.[32]

The legacies of A. D. Williams, his locally famous son-in-law, and his internationally famous grandson provide a connection to historic rural Black congregations and churches, some of which stand while others have vanished. The Bethabara Baptist Church from the nineteenth century is gone, though a newer cinder-block church with the same name still stands nearby. There is no minutes book documenting the congregation's comings and goings, noting the rising prospects of preachers like Williams as the community came to see their calling, or exposing the intrigue between church members. There is no building one might walk through and imagine the congregation at worship or business. The cemetery continues to endure the slow reforesting of its buried members, covering over the rich history of this place's past. Even if the prospects of the church were harsh in 1900, there were people keeping watch over its living and dead. The decline of the congregation and loss of the church building denote a larger change in rural American life.

Rural religious spaces are vulnerable. The Historic Rural Churches of Georgia project is a testament to their value, not just to the history of Georgia but for the powerful stories they can tell us about American religious history. Even if the white congregations in this collection

The old road to Bethabara winds through tall stands of trees. A timber company now owns the property where the church used to sit.

have a better footprint to retell their stories, they too are at the mercy of dwindling membership and financial resources. It is not enough to mark this moment with a retelling of these churches; we must work together to provide resources to more fully understand how ancestors built their lives around the hope for a better life, if not for themselves then for their children's children. We hope this introduction and collection call all of us to comb the past to better understand the historic rural roots of religious life in Georgia.

NOTES

1. E. Franklin Frazier, *The Negro Church in America*, and C. Eric Lincoln, *The Black Church since Frazier* (New York: Schocken Books, 1974), 13.

2. Gayraud S. Wilmore, *Black Religion and Black Radicalism* (New York: Doubleday, 1972), 5, 8, 9.

3. Frazier, *Negro Church in America*, 13.

4. Lawrence W. Levine, *Black Culture and Black Consciousness* (New York: Oxford University Press, 1977), 57.

5. W. E. B. Du Bois, *The Souls of Black Folk* (New York: Bantam Books, 1989), 138. For a fuller explication of the melding of African worldviews with Christian myths, see Noel Leo Erskine, *Plantation Church: How African American Religion Was Born in Caribbean Slavery* (New York: Oxford University Press, 2014).

6. Yolanda Y. Smith, *Reclaiming the Spirituals* (Cleveland: Pilgrim Press, 2004), 69.

7. Herbert S. Klein, *Slavery in the Americas* (Chicago: University of Chicago Press, 1967), 120.

8. James Melvin Washington, *Frustrated Fellowship: The Black Baptist Quest for Social Power* (Macon, Ga.: Mercer University Press, 1990), 8.

9. See Charles O. Walker, "Georgia's Religion in the Colonial Era, 1733–1790," *Viewpoints: Georgia Baptist History* 5 (1976): 33.

10. John Palmer Gates, "George Liele: A Pioneer Negro Preacher," *Chronicle: A Baptist Historical Quarterly* 6, no. 3 (July 1943): 120. Quotation marks in the above citation may be confusing. Gates cites John Rippon of *The Baptist Annual Register*, who received original letters from Liele. Rippon explains that he edited Liele's letters with quotation marks bracketing the original sections of Liele's letters.

11. John Rippon, *The Baptist Annual Register for 1790, 1791, 1792, and Part of 1793*, vol. 1 (London: n.p., n.d.), 332–33.

12. E. Brooks Holifield, *Theology in America: Christian Thought from the Age of the Puritans to the Civil War* (New Haven, Conn.: Yale University Press, 2003), 310. See also Rippon, *Baptist Annual Register*, 336.

13. See "The Covenant of the Anabaptist Church: Begun in America December 1777, and in Jamaica, December 1783," 1796, British Baptist material, Angus Library of Regents Park College, Oxford, England, reel 1, no. 14; publication (Historical Commission, Southern Baptist Convention), MF 4265. Writing from Jamaica, Liele produced a church covenant with twenty-one articles that linked churches in Georgia and Jamaica. For a full description, see Erskine, *Plantation Church*, 172–181.

14. See Holifield, *Theology in America*.

15. Dr. Walter H. Brooks (1851–1945) was a well-known minister, leader, and scholar in the Black Baptist Church.

16. Carter G. Woodson, *The History of the Negro Church* (Washington, D.C.: Associated Publishers, 1921), 43.

17. See Walker, "Georgia's Religion," 34. In my research in Jamaica I have been unable to find any trace of Matthew Moore's presence.

18. Penfield Baptist Church Minutes Book, 66, Special Collections, Jack Tarver Library, Mercer University, Macon, Georgia, https://hdl.handle.net/10898/10041.

19. Douglas E. Thompson, "Educating Mastery: Mercer University, Baptist Education, and the Penfield Experiment," *Perspectives in Religious Studies* 50, no. 4 (Winter 2023): 417–30.

20. Penfield Baptist Church Minutes Book, 57, 61.

21. *Athens Weekly Banner*, May 20, 1890, 7, Georgia Historic Newspapers, https://gahistoricnewspapers.galileo.usg.edu/lccn/sn88054117/1890-05-20/ed-1/seq-7/#date1=01%2F01%2F1890¬text=&date2=12%2F31%2F1890&words=Shoals+shoals+Skull+skull&searchType=advanced&sequence=0&index=0&proxdistance=5&rows=12&ortext=&proxtext=skull+shoals&andtext=&page=1.

22. C. Eric Lincoln and Lawrence H. Mamiya, *The Black Church in the African American Experience* (Durham, N.C.: Duke University Press, 1990), 96–97.

23. Penfield Baptist Church Minutes Book, 60–61.

24. Ibid., 94.

25. Ibid., 119.

26. "Shiloh Baptist Church Minutes," November 1, 1846, and October 15, 1855, cited in *The Papers of Martin Luther King, Jr.*, vol. 1: *Called to Serve, January 1929–June 1951*, ed. Clayborne Carson (Berkeley: University of California Press, 1992), 2.

27. U.S. Census, 1870, Georgia, Greene County, District 148 (Penfield).

28. U.S. Census, 1880, Georgia, Greene County, June 15, 1880.

29. *Greensboro Herald*, November 27, 1873, 2, Georgia Historic Newspapers, https://gahistoricnewspapers.galileo.usg.edu/lccn/sn85034053/1873-11-27/ed-1/seq-2/.

30. Greene County, Georgia, Tax Digest, 1870–1873.

31. "Introduction," in Carson, *Papers of Martin Luther King, Jr.*, 5–6.

32. "Introduction," in Carson, *Papers of Martin Luther King, Jr.*, 6–7.

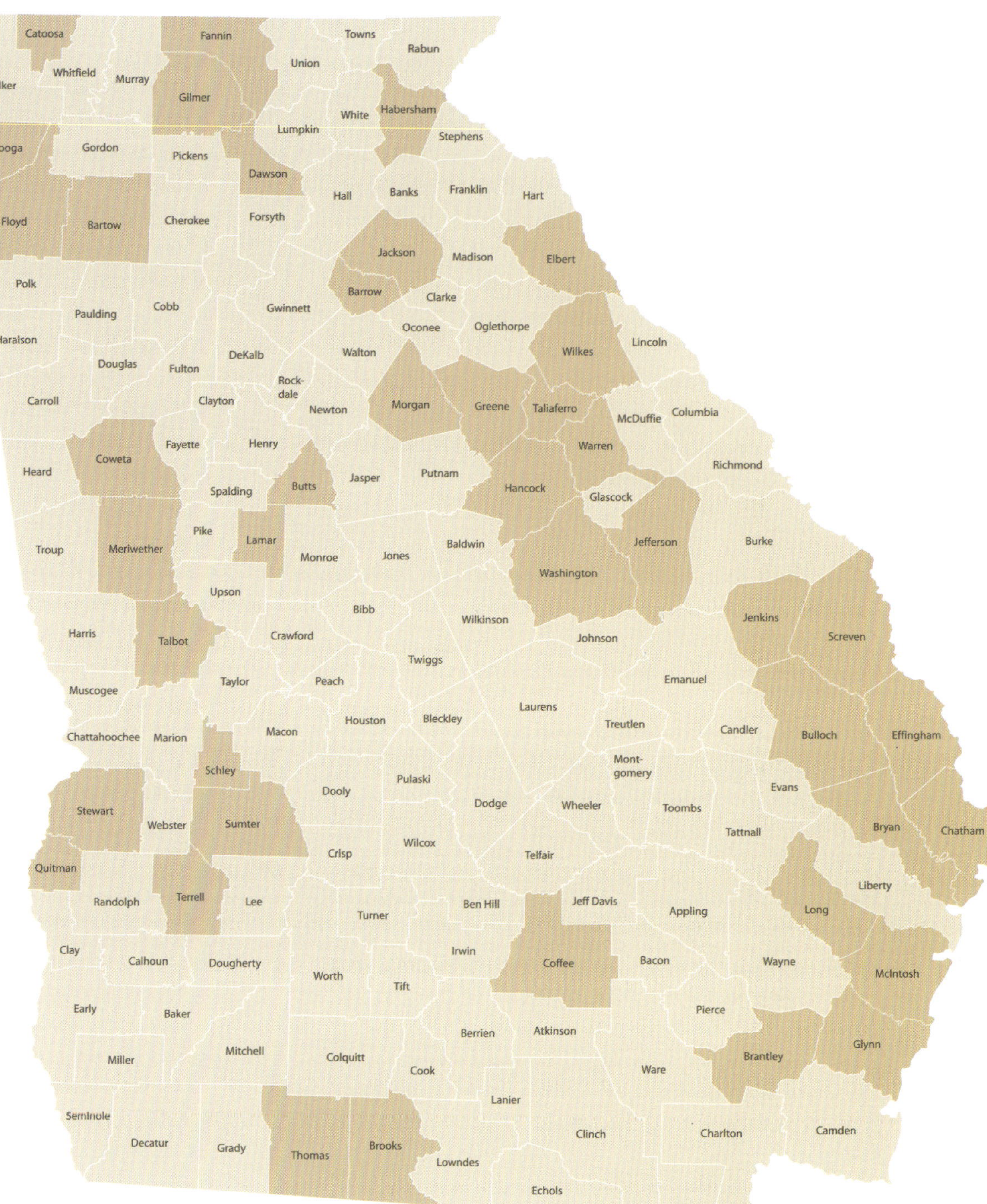

Barrow	*Rockwell Universalist*
Bartow	*Mount Carmel Methodist*
Brantley	*Bethlehem Primitive Baptist*
Brooks	*Grooverville Methodist*
Bryan	*Bryan Neck Presbyterian*
Bulloch	*Union Methodist*
Butts	*Indian Springs Baptist*
Catoosa	*Old Stone Church*
Chatham	*St. Bartholomew's Episcopal*
Chattooga	*Bethel Presbyterian*
Coffee	*Cumorah Church of Latter-day Saints*
Coweta	*White Oak Presbyterian*
Dawson	*Lumpkin Campground*
Effingham	*Mizpah Methodist*
Elbert	*Ruckersville Methodist*
Fannin	*Tarpley Chapel*
Floyd	*Chubb Chapel Methodist*
Floyd	*Glendale Chapel Methodist*
Floyd	*Possum Trot Church*
Gilmer	*Ridgeway Baptist*
Glynn	*Good Shepherd Episcopal*
Glynn	*Needwood Baptist*
Greene	*Siloam Presbyterian*
Habersham	*Mount Airy Presbyterian*
Hancock	*Mount Zion Presbyterian*
Hancock	*Rock Mills Methodist*
Jackson	*Academy Baptist*
Jefferson	*Ways Grove Baptist*
Jenkins	*Fair Haven Methodist*
Lamar	*Union Primitive Baptist*
Long	*Walthourville Presbyterian*
McIntosh	*St. Andrew's Episcopal*
McIntosh	*Wayfair Primitive Baptist*
Meriwether	*Odessadale Methodist*
Morgan	*Swords Methodist*
Quitman	*Hopewell Missionary Baptist*
Schley	*Phillippi Primitive Baptist*
Screven	*Bethel Brick Methodist*
Screven	*Walker Grove Baptist*
Stewart	*Providence Methodist*
Sumter	*Friendship Baptist*
Talbot	*Corinth Methodist*
Talbot	*Zion Episcopal*
Taliaferro	*Sharon Methodist*
Terrell	*Red Hill AME*
Thomas	*Bethany Congregational*
Thomas	*Springhill Methodist*
Warren	*Williams Creek Baptist*
Washington	*Antioch Baptist*
Wilkes	*Phillips Mill Baptist*

More Historic Rural Churches of Georgia

PHOTOGRAPHY BY RANDY CLEGG

Rockwell Universalist

BARROW COUNTY ORG. 1839

Located in what was known as the Mulberry community, Rockwell Universalist was initially organized in 1839 as the First Universalist Church of Jackson County. According to the historical marker at the site, Rockwell is the second oldest Universalist church in Georgia. The church met first in a brush arbor and later on the first floor of a two-story building across the road. The first floor was used as a local school—the Rockwell School—and the upper story as a Masonic lodge. The school and Masonic lodge also functioned as a recruiting and training location for soldiers during the Civil War, as well as a justice court and a voting precinct for what was known as House's District.

The church building seen here was erected in 1881 using volunteer labor and donated materials from the community. At the dedication, it was renamed the Mulberry Church. In the 1920s, its name changed again, this time to Rockwell, in recognition of the school and Masonic hall where its members had worshipped for so many years.

Many Universalist state conventions were held at Rockwell. Prior to one of these conventions, in 1895, the church was finished inside with a ceiling and interior features using lumber donated by one of its members. The historical character of the church has been well maintained over the years, even as development and highways have encroached on the area. Rockwell Universalist was added to the National Register of Historic Places in 1985.

Founding member John G. House (also spelled Howse and Howze) was the local justice of the peace and schoolmaster. He and his wife, Margaret, had nine children, including four sons who served in the Civil War. Two of them did not survive. Of the sixty-one graves in the nearby House Cemetery, thirty-one carry the surname House or Howse. The House family roots are very deep in what was then Jackson County and is now Barrow County.

Although the sanctuary of Rockwell Universalist has been modified and improved many times since its initial construction, the interior design, layout, and decorative elements remain true to its original character. Today it still presents as a cozy, attractive, nineteenth-century rural church.

This view from the pulpit illustrates the sanctuary's compact design that packs members of the congregation closely together and brings them right up to the chancel.

Tall, nine-by-nine, double-hung, frosted-glass windows flood the interior with natural light. According to church records, the original, primitive pews were replaced around 1905 or 1906. The pews shown here were handmade.

The grave of John G. House (Howze) (1805–62), the patriarch of the family, is in the foreground. Beside him is the grave of his wife, Margaret (1813–69), and beyond them is that of Missourie House, a daughter who died in 1876, at the age of nineteen. The engravings on the stones showcase the alternative spellings of the family name.

The two stacked-stone graves are those of Mary J. and James L., both infants who died before their first birthday. At the foot of each is a marble marker in tribute to two of John G.'s sons, William and Henry. Both died of disease in Richmond during the Civil War.

PHOTOGRAPHY BY TOM REED

Mount Carmel Methodist

BARTOW COUNTY ORG. 1847

According to a church history written in 1955, people living in the communities of Rockdodger, Hall's Station, and Linwood organized the Mount Carmel Methodist Church in 1847. Many of the early members came from the Kingston Methodist Church located nearby. The original church was a log house, but in 1856, Robert Nelson Kerr donated land and the first frame structure was built between the present drive and the cemetery.

The church history noted the rear of the building was designated for enslaved people who came to worship. Some African Americans continued to attend after emancipation. Services were held on both Saturday and Sunday, with congregants arriving on horseback or in ox carts.

The courthouse at Cassville was burned during the Civil War and all the records were lost, including the title for Robert Kerr's 1856 donation to the church. According to the church history, in 1891 J. C. Kerr deeded to the church trustees the 2 acres of land his father had originally donated to be used for a church and graveyard.

The church prospered after the war, and a new sanctuary, the present one, was constructed in 1903, using some labor and materials donated by members. Lumber for the floors and ceiling came by rail from Dalton, while the windows and doors arrived in wagons from Rome. Electricity was installed in 1947.

Many older rural church sanctuaries have undergone occasional upgrades that altered the interior. By contrast, with the exception of a few modern additions such as ceiling fans, Mount Carmel looks almost exactly as it did in the first decade of the twentieth century.

This close-up of the chancel and pulpit area shows the vertical wainscoting and horizontal wallboards are all made of narrow-gauge wood. This is decidedly a trend of the late Victorian era; in earlier times, wider lumber would have been used. The heavy turned balusters and colorful, high, Gothic windows are also characteristic of the period.

This view from the pulpit reveals another trend of the late Victorian era—the ceiling design and finish. In this era, it became popular to soften the juncture of wall and ceiling by employing narrow horizontal boards, allowing the walls above the ceiling molding to curve gracefully into the ceiling.

PHOTOGRAPHY BY RANDALL DAVIS

Bethlehem Primitive Baptist

BRANTLEY COUNTY ORG. 1880

Located in Brantley County, Bethlehem is one of those southeast Georgia churches belonging to the Wiregrass Primitive Baptist sect, an unusual, little known, and fascinating part of early Georgia religious history. The architecture and design of their churches are representative of an all-encompassing, conservative approach to life and religion. This religious sect was prolific in southeast Georgia and parts of northern Florida in the early 1800s. The sect continues to the present day, although in much smaller numbers. Much of what we learned about the Wiregrass Primitive ritual services came from lifelong member and elder Nathan Deal.

We also gleaned information from John Crowley's book *Primitive Baptists of the Wiregrass South: 1815 to the Present*, first published in 1998. According to Crowley, the region's land was not suitable for agriculture, and the people who settled there were largely Scots-Irish stock drovers who hunted and raised wild cattle. They were characterized as fiercely independent and they kept to themselves. Many of their neighbors in the region were not aware of them at all.

The churches were built on site of native materials with local church labor and therefore vary slightly from building to building. However, the basic design and floor plan were always the same—no paint, no steeple, no window treatments, no distinct doors or entry points. No pianos or organs were allowed, yet the members loved to sing and, according to Crowley, singing formed an important part of worship. One of the most common forms of this a cappella singing is known as "lined out hymns," in which the preacher or a singing clerk leads the congregation one or two lines at a time. This early practice allowed a congregation to have a single hymnbook and made it easier for illiterate members to participate.

We are not certain of the exact date of organization for Bethlehem. We know that the church joined the Alabaha River Association of Primitive Baptists (Crawford faction) in 1905, but some headstones in the church cemetery are from much earlier. We estimated Bethlehem's founding date of 1880 based on the oldest marked grave in the church cemetery, which bears a death date of 1881.

Because it was sandy and poorly suited for agriculture, the Wiregrass Region was sparsely populated. It was not far from the coastal rice kings and wealthy planters, yet seemed to be another world. Crowley's book refers to a Georgia legislative committee sent to inspect a stretch of Wiregrass land acquired by the Native American cessations of 1814 and 1818. The committee advised it would be "unwise to spend the people's money trying to develop a country which God Almighty himself had left in an unfinished condition."

The church and the cemetery are managed by a board of local citizens, who are helping to maintain this important part of Georgia history. Their preservation efforts include a metal roof and pole shed for the water pump.

The typical design of a Primitive Baptist church included an aisle from the front door to the stand (the pulpit), intersected by a second aisle between the two end doors. Elders were the only members allowed to enter the stand. The short bench in front of the stand was for the use of the clerk and the moderator. Beneath the communion table is a hole in the floor, to serve as a funnel for the disposal of water used in the foot-washing ritual.

In this view looking from the stand toward the double front doors, the cemetery can be seen in the distance. Elderly men sat on the left side of the stand and elderly women on the right. The general congregation sat on the benches in front of the stand.

This gracefully constructed bench placed inside the stand was for the use of the elders. Deacons decide who will occupy the stand on a given day. They believe that when they go out to the church yard "to inquire who should stand," God appoints the elder who will go in the pulpit that day. Elders do not prepare sermons or use outlines or notes of any kind. All of it is extemporaneous.

Primitive Baptist churches in the Wiregrass are built on heart pine wooden footings resting on top of sand. Because the soil drains quickly, wooden footings are all that is required. The middle window is elevated to accommodate the raised floor of the stand where the elders preach. The large cemetery, containing 797 interments, is visible beside the church.

Grave houses have become rare in today's landscape, and this is one of the finest examples we have located. We don't know the identity of those interred within as their grave markers were made of wood, and any identifying inscriptions have long since faded.

PHOTOGRAPHY BY STEVE ROBINSON

Grooverville Methodist

BROOKS COUNTY ORG. 1856

Situated in a peaceful spot on a tree-shaded dirt road, Grooverville Methodist is only a few yards away from another historic church—Liberty Baptist (featured in volume 1). These two structures attest to the vibrancy of the little village of Grooverville that was located on the stage road from Tallahassee to Thomasville.

Grooverville Methodist Church began as a brush-arbor meeting place on the property of William H. Ramsey—an ancestor of Clay Ramsey, whose 2017 article in *Georgia Backroads* magazine provided much of our source history about the church. In 1832, the Ramsey family moved from Bladen County, North Carolina, to Thomas (later Brooks) County, Georgia. Without an established church in the area and anxious to worship according to Methodist practice, William Ramsey began services for his family and slaves in a temporary shelter on his land. As families with Methodist convictions gradually settled in the area, they sought out others with similar religious affinities and decided a sturdier structure should be built, which they named Lebanon Church.

Eventually, the members of Lebanon Church decided to move their congregation to the growing town of Grooverville, and they were granted an acre of land by property owner Malachi Groover. With the move, the church changed its name to reflect its new location.

Shuttered windows and a belfry, with sides of wide planks painted white, mark the modest style of the church. At one time, it was the largest congregation on a circuit that included Grooverville, Beulah, and Prospect. Church members stopped meeting in the 1990s and the building fell into disrepair, but recently there have been some renovation efforts. It remains in a quiet stand of pine as perhaps the oldest church building in Brooks County.

These nine-over-nine sashed windows remain in working order after decades of use. The condition of the church's siding, window frames, and shutters demonstrates the toughness, rot resistance, and durability of the longleaf pine wood indigenous to the area.

To the left of the piano are the original, simple pews in the choir area. The addition of the gas stove in the twentieth century probably made the congregation more comfortable than the potbellied stove it replaced.

This view is a rare sight—a pre–Civil War rural church that has stood virtually unchanged for over 150 years. Horizontal wall boards and vertical ceiling boards create a subtle effect and are the interior's only decorative elements.

The windows were designed to give abundant ambient light, and perhaps a warming ray of sun in the winter. In the summer, the windows could be raised.

The chancel and the raised pulpit are simple but classic in design. The elaborate railing frames the chancel and gives a dignified presence to the pulpit. It is unusual to find double doors of this type at the rear of the church; normally a double entrance is in the front.

Decades after it was last used for worship services, Grooverville is showing its age. The belfry is battered, though it could easily be resurrected. Cornice returns, shutters, and the roof need repair. The stock fences around the foundation need mending but otherwise are in remarkable condition.

PHOTOGRAPHY BY WAYNE MOORE

Bryan Neck Presbyterian

BRYAN COUNTY ORG. 1830

Bryan Neck Presbyterian was located in one of the richest rice-growing areas on the Eastern Seaboard, and its congregation reaped the financial benefits from a planter class that dominated the rice trade. These "rice kings" were some of the wealthiest people in America and included such families as the Clays, Maxwells, Arnolds, Rogerses, and McAllisters. Thousands of acres were under cultivation, worked by one of the largest slave populations on the Georgia coast.

According to Kenneth Krakow in his *Georgia Place-Names*, "Bryan Neck was the name given to a narrow, lower part of the county between the Great Ogeechee and Midway Rivers." The land, with its endless flow of fresh water from the two rivers, was perfect for growing rice. The planters who settled there in the eighteenth century prospered for generations thanks to their available land, water, and slave labor. The rice production peaked, according to the Richmond Hill Historical Society, in 1860 when the Bryan Neck plantations along the Ogeechee produced 1.6 million pounds.

Bryan Neck Presbyterian was established by several of the planter class families in November 1830 with the official sanction of the Savannah Presbytery and with assistance from the Congregational church at Midway, with which some of the families had previously been affiliated. The congregation used a former Episcopal church building until a new building was dedicated in 1841. A wooden frame structure with two entrances, a belfry, and a slave gallery, it served the community for over forty years until it was destroyed by fire in 1882. Services resumed under the leadership of members Habersham Clay and C. C. Maxwell.

Maxwell and Clay ultimately bought land for the current church in 1885, approximately two miles from the original site, and furnished money for its construction. The church is unusual in its size, architectural configuration, and interior finishes. The present congregation has done a remarkable job of maintaining the original structure.

The church graveyard, known as Burnt Church Cemetery, is located at the original 1831 church site and includes the family plots of early church leaders, such as the McAllisters and Clays. Thomas Savage Clay was a devout Presbyterian who was well known in the denomination for promoting "religious instruction" for enslaved people on Bryan Neck plantations.

In 2000 the church was placed on the National Register of Historic Places, which supplied much of the above history.

This small, inviting masterpiece epitomizes the expression *jewel box*. The most recognizable feature is the tongue-and-groove wood paneling that is presented in many decorative patterns. These panels are varnished from floor to ceiling and create a warm glowing light throughout the space.

The decorative power of the diverse paneling at Bryan Neck Presbyterian is particularly evident in the apse behind the altar. The clear-glass windows on each side focus light onto it. The diamond in the middle sits amid converging diagonal boards, creating a bull's-eye effect that draws attention to that spot.

To the left is one of two school rooms that are sited at the ends of the east and west arms of the cross-shaped sanctuary. The rooms could be closed off from the sanctuary by folding wood-and-glass doors.

This view, looking north into the second classroom, illustrates the high-quality fit and finish of the woodwork.

In its small corner, the old pump organ blends with rich floors, vertical wainscoting, and herringbone wall paneling.

Burnt Church Cemetery, at the original site of the Bryan Neck Presbyterian Church, contains multiple graves of the Clay family—including Thomas Savage Clay, a founding member of the church, who died in 1849. Also interred here is George Washington McAllister, one of the largest slave owners in the area. His 1838 plantation home, Strathy Hall, was restored by Henry Ford in 1940.

PHOTOGRAPHY BY RANDALL DAVIS

Union Methodist

BULLOCH COUNTY ORG. 1790

Union Methodist, in deep rural Bulloch County, has been in continuous service for well over two hundred years at this site. The church was organized in 1790, making it the oldest Methodist church in the county and one of the oldest in Georgia. The church was first organized in the home of Joshua Hodges, a Revolutionary War soldier who served in the Martin County, North Carolina, militia. He was given land grants in Georgia for his war service and settled in Bulloch County, where he became a successful planter.

According to the website of the denomination's South Georgia Conference, the first structure on the site was a log meetinghouse, built in 1791. In 1834, a new building was erected, which the website describes as "made of planks [and sitting] off of the ground on log pillars with a steep roof and four evenly spaced windows." This building was then replaced in 1884 by the present structure. According to Union tradition, some of the pews and parts of the altar rail came from the 1834 sanctuary.

At the time of the Civil War, many of the church records were dispersed among the membership for safekeeping. The records placed with the Porter family have survived, including some membership rolls. Although this part of Georgia was not dominated by large plantations at the time of the war, there were African American members in the church. The 1844 rolls, for instance, show there were five white males, fifteen white females, and five Black members.

Union Church would always remain small because of its location. It was solely dependent on local families who farmed in the area, which makes its survival even more remarkable. Renovation efforts, led by the Hodges family, are ongoing. The Hodges family still has deep roots in the area.

The interior of the church reflects the congregation's conservative and simple taste. There is minimal interior decoration or ornamentation. The center pews date from the 1834 church and have mortised notches indicating the separation of men from women and children in the sanctuary—a common practice in the early nineteenth century.

Imagine how large the longleaf pine tree had to be to produce the single-board planks used to make these pews. The widths range from 18 to 24 inches, indicating a trunk diameter as large as 4 feet—a pine tree size not seen in the forests of Georgia since the nineteenth century.

The clear-glass six-over-six windows allow the little sanctuary to glow while providing a view of the Bulloch County landscape. Union Methodist has provided spiritual comfort in these surroundings for more than two hundred years.

This old outhouse remains on the church premises, a reminder of days gone by.

The oldest grave in the cemetery is that of Joshua's wife, Ann Raiford Hodges, who died in 1795. Of the ninety-six documented interments in the cemetery, twenty-eight are from the Hodges family. Members of the family have continuously served the church for over two centuries.

PHOTOGRAPHY BY TONY CANTRELL

Indian Springs Baptist

BUTTS COUNTY ORG. 1825

Indian Springs Baptist in Butts County was originally a log church established in 1825. It was subsequently replaced by a frame building in 1854. The present sanctuary is a beautiful example of late nineteenth-century Queen Anne craftsmanship, made from leftover lumber and construction material used to build the famous Wigwam Hotel in 1890. The Wigwam was a four-story Victorian structure, said to be one of the largest frame buildings in the world at that time.

The history of Indian Springs goes back hundreds of years. Once home to members of the Creek Nation, the area was well known among Indigenous people for the life-giving elements of its sulfur springs. As white settlers moved in, conflict with the Creeks became rampant due to the relentless push westward by state and federal authorities to eliminate Indigenous people and acquire their land. In 1790 a treaty was signed whereby Georgia acquired the land between the Ogeechee and Oconee Rivers. In 1804 another treaty ceded the land between the Oconee and Ocmulgee Rivers. In 1821, the first treaty of Indian Springs was negotiated, which ceded the land between the Ocmulgee and Flint Rivers.

William McIntosh, a chief of the Lower Creeks, was one of the primary signatories to the 1821 treaty, and he profited from it by acquiring substantial land around the springs. He then built the Indian Springs Hotel in 1823, which still stands across from the entrance to Indian Springs State Park. The hotel has been fully restored and is open to the public.

In 1825, McIntosh and his allies signed a second treaty, ceding the remaining Creek land between the Flint River and the Chattahoochee. From the perspective of white settlers, the final push to the Chattahoochee River on the Alabama border was now completed. However, the Creek leadership council maintained that McIntosh did not have the authority to sign such a treaty and condemned him to death. The sentence was swiftly enforced. On April 29, the Upper Creek chief Menewa took two hundred warriors to attack McIntosh at his plantation on the Chattahoochee River in present-day Carroll County. They killed him and two other signatories and set fire to the house.

As these former Creek lands were added to the growing state of Georgia, one outcome was the establishment of land lots around the springs. Georgia's government directed that these lots be held in perpetuity as a public recreation area, thus making Indian Springs the oldest state-owned recreation area in the country. Resort hotels were built, some with as many as seven hundred rooms.

The Butts County Historical Society is the primary source for the church's history. It also maintains the church building.

Indian Springs Baptist, built in the 1890s, features pews to the left and right of the aisle, as well as a simple but dramatic apse for the raised chancel and pulpit. All the furnishings, wainscoting, and trim reflect superior craftsmanship.

Next to the chancel and nestled in a corner near the choir area is a handsome and rare Victorian pump organ. This organ stood in the Carmichael House in Jackson, Georgia, for many years and was recently placed in the chapel's sanctuary.

In the main sanctuary of the church are ten pews of the length seen here, while eight longer pews are placed elsewhere. The Butts County Historical Society believes that the pews pictured here are much older than the building itself and may have been saved from another church.

This large, well-crafted bench sits in the back of the apse behind the pulpit. The size and craftsmanship style are well proportioned for the sanctuary.

This view from the pulpit displays the unusual configuration of the sanctuary, with the main entrance on the far right. The rear wall is nearly covered with colorful stained-glass windows.

There are 102 documented interments in the cemetery and almost certainly some that are unmarked. Half of the recorded graves are from the nineteenth century, with the oldest being that of James A. Saunders, an infant who died in 1845.

PHOTOGRAPHY BY TOM REED

Old Stone Church

CATOOSA COUNTY ORG. 1837

The Old Stone Church was originally organized in 1837 as the Chickamauga Presbyterian Church. Its meetings were held first in a log schoolhouse approximately one-quarter of a mile south of its current location, and later in a small frame house. Construction of the present structure began in the summer of 1850. Stone was hauled by charter church member Robert Magill and his two brothers, from a nearby quarry at White Oak Mountain. The building was completed in 1852 at a cost of $1,600, part of which was donated by the Reverend W. H. Johnston, who gave his yearly salary of $200.

The building is architecturally significant in that it is made of native sandstone from a local quarry. We think it is probably the state's only sandstone sanctuary built before the Civil War. The pews and the altar are original, and the nearby cemetery contains the graves of many of Catoosa County's first white settlers.

This northwest section of Georgia was part of the Cherokee Nation in the early 1800s, but gold was discovered in north Georgia in 1829, bringing in thousands of fortune hunters. The state took control of the land in 1831 with the creation of Cherokee County, which was subdivided into ten counties in 1832. Parcels of land were then distributed to white settlers in the Cherokee land lottery of 1832. Ultimately the Cherokees were forcefully removed to the Oklahoma Territory in 1838 in what became known as the Trail of Tears.

During the Civil War, there was conflict in the area as federal troops advanced from Chattanooga toward Atlanta. In the Battle of Ringgold Gap in late November 1863, Union general Joseph Hooker fought Confederates under the command of

General Patrick Cleburne just north of the church. The following May, according to the National Register of Historic Places, federal brigadier general Judson Kilpatrick "reported . . . that he met the Confederates one mile from 'Stone Church' . . . and drove them to Tunnell Hill." Tradition maintains that the church served as a hospital for wounded soldiers on both sides, and that blood stains are still visible on the floor.

The building was known as Chickamauga Presbyterian until 1912, when its name changed to Stone Church due to a naming conflict with another church. The Presbyterians ceased to use the building in 1921, and it was then purchased by the Methodists. The building changed ownership several times and is now owned by the Catoosa County Historical Society, which uses it as their headquarters as well as for a museum. In 1979, the church was placed on the National Register of Historic Places.

The thickness of the church walls becomes apparent when we see the deep setback of the windows in this view from the pulpit. The walls were laid in an irregular pattern with stones of various sizes.

Even though the pews have been painted, wavy plane marks are visible in the wood—evidence that the pews were made by hand. The wide floorboards show marks of many years of use.

Though the church now serves as the headquarters and museum of the Catoosa County Historical Society, its sanctuary looks much as it did when it was constructed in 1852. The original pews rest sturdily on the same heart pine floors. The chancel, altar balustrade, and pulpit are original as well.

PHOTOGRAPHY BY WAYNE MOORE

St. Bartholomew's Episcopal

CHATHAM COUNTY ORG. 1896

St. Bartholomew's Episcopal is one of the most historically significant African American churches in Georgia, with roots dating back to the 1830s, when approximately one thousand enslaved people worked in the rice fields on several large plantations nearby.

According to the National Register of Historic Places,

> in 1832, Episcopal religious education for slaves in this area was initiated by a white family on their plantation. In 1845, the Ogeechee Mission was formally established when, in an effort to reach out to the slaves, the Episcopal bishop appointed the first permanent pastor to the area. This priest, Rev. William C. Williams, was to join contiguous plantations under his ministry, live in the area and become the slaves' pastor. Williams established a school and a chapel on each of the three plantations he then served. His success with the slaves was such that by 1860 his congregation was the largest, black or white, in the Episcopal Diocese of Georgia.

Prior to the Civil War, slaves were allowed to attend their masters' church but rarely permitted to form their own. African American Episcopal churches are rare in Georgia, and most are in the coastal region. In the early 1800s, plantations moved inland as cotton began to replace rice as the most important cash crop. The predominant denominations that emerged in the Georgia backcountry were Baptist and Methodist and, to a lesser extent, Presbyterian.

St. Bartholomew's, located in the village of Burroughs, is the oldest continuing Black congregation in the Episcopal Diocese of Georgia. Following the Civil War, Burroughs was established as a settlement of former slaves, who were given the opportunity to buy land from their former owners. In 1881, St. Bartholomew's Church in New York City gave $400 to the Burroughs mission congregation for a new schoolhouse and church. The new church adopted the name of its patron congregation and was consecrated in 1896, with the school building completed the following year.

St. Bartholomew's, which had over four hundred members at its peak in the early 1900s, is still active with a few members today. In 1982 it was placed on the National Register of Historic Places, which is the source for much of the above history.

The church's architecture reflects the late Victorian era, with a square bell tower, Gothic windows, and fanciful decorative elements.

This is the oldest continuing Black congregation in the Episcopal Diocese of Georgia. The fit and finish of elements in the sanctuary are superior to those in most of the rural churches we feature.

EXIT

There are significant differences between St. Bartholomew's and other rural African American churches of its era. The fact that it is still supported by the Episcopal Church and received its early financing from a wealthy New York congregation is reflected in its design, furnishings, and decorative elements.

In this view, the relatively large size of the church interior becomes apparent. The simple pews sit on the original heart pine floorboards just as they have for decades. The sanctuary was designed to accommodate about two hundred, and we are told it was often filled to capacity in days gone by.

PHOTOGRAPHY BY RANDY CLEGG

Bethel Presbyterian

CHATTOOGA COUNTY ORG. 1847

The history of Bethel Presbyterian is, to a great extent, the history of the northwest Georgia mountains and the sturdy Scots-Irish pioneers who settled so much of it after the Cherokee removals. It is also the story of the Armuchee Academy, the Reverend T. C. Crawford, and Bethel Yard, a burial ground containing interments going as far back as 1838.

The church sits in a lovely rural setting in the north Georgia mountains, just as it has since it was built in 1847 on land acquired in the Cherokee land lottery by Augustus Bryant. It was here that Crawford came from North Carolina to establish a church and a school. He was a man of letters who graduated from Davidson College as salutatorian and attended Columbia Theological Seminary. In addition to forming a church he established Armuchee Academy, the first high school in Chattooga County, which attracted students from as far away as Alabama and Tennessee. Both the school and the church prospered, and in 1849, construction began on the simple clapboard sanctuary you see here.

Of the 291 documented interments in Bethel Yard, twenty-seven are Civil War veterans—a remarkably high concentration in a single church community. Reverend Crawford is buried here, too, as are the McSpadden brothers, murdered by a band of Union scouts who hunted down Confederate soldiers and sympathizers. Also lying in the church cemetery is the enslaved Cyrus Jenkins Vance, who served with his master on many battlefields, including two occasions when his enslaver was wounded, and was ultimately at his deathbed. Vance served surviving family members all the way to Appomattox, finally returning home to live out his days nearby on the original family farm.

Information for our commentary comes from various county sources and newspaper articles and particularly from *Bethel Presbyterian Church: Dirt Town, Chattooga County, Georgia* by local historian Thomas Weaver Weesner.

How many hymns have been sung, weddings performed, sermons preached, and eulogies delivered in this sacred place? Bethel served its community for over 150 years.

This view from the pulpit remains virtually unchanged since 1849. After its congregation shrank to fewer than five members, Bethel ceased operations as a Presbyterian church.

A 2005 *Chattanooga Press* article by Louise McCollum paid tribute to Rev. T. C. Crawford's legacy. McCollum quoted from church historian Sam Jones, who wrote, "As a result of the church and school in this community, there have gone out fourteen ministers of the Gospel, fourteen doctors of medicine, two foreign missionaries, more than a hundred school teachers, five state senators, five representatives to the Georgia legislature, one superior court judge, and hundreds of good, moral Christian men and women in the business world."

The graveyard at Bethel is one of the most picturesque cemeteries in the Georgia high country, with many stories to tell. Nearly 10 percent of the documented graves belong to Civil War veterans.

A poem on the Bethel church wall reads:

In this quiet city of the dead
Lie faithful women, men well-read
Who bravely fought for truth and right.
And gallantly they won their fight
Ere they went down.

The stone wall may crumble and decay,
But the influence of these who went away
Will never die,
Although they lie
In Bethel Yard.

Sleep on ye brave, nor heed the strife
And fury of the modern life.
The Sabbath breaker or infidel
Shall wake you not, for all is well.
Sleep peacefully, for all is well.

Your flaming torch aloft we bear.
With burning heart and vow, we swear
To keep the faith and fight it through,
To crush the foe, then sleep with you
In Bethel Yard.

One of the many tragic stories of the Civil War in this part of Georgia involved two brothers, Ernest and Christopher McSpadden, who worked as Confederate scouts in the Chattooga-Walker area. During the latter part of the war, renegade gangs representing both sides of the conflict roamed the Georgia hills at will with little or no official sanction. On the Union side, a group known as the John Long–Sam Roberts gang hunted down Ernest and Christopher in the nearby community of Dirt Town, where they were murdered. Reverend Crawford officiated over the McSpadden brothers' burial in Bethel Yard.

PHOTOGRAPHY BY CYNTHIA JENNINGS

Cumorah Church of Latter-day Saints

COFFEE COUNTY ORG. 1907

Though it looked like an aging, abandoned farmhouse sitting in a field next to a large pond, Cumorah Church of Latter-day Saints (LDS) was until 2024 actually the oldest standing Mormon church in Georgia. It was built in 1907 on two acres of land in Coffee County donated by Joseph Adams, one of the earliest LDS converts in the state.

Cumorah was the second Mormon church established in south Georgia. The first, known as Little Utah, was organized in 1907 about twenty miles away, near the town of Axson. Like Cumorah, it no longer stands, but for many years, Cumorah and Little Utah were the only two Mormon churches in south Georgia. A few years before its destruction, Cumorah was moved to its final location from its original site by the church cemetery a short distance away. The *Cumorah Junction* blog notes that Cumorah "was used by the Douglas Latter-day Saints up until 1961 when the current chapel was built. It received some renovation in 1935 to add space for a stage and classrooms. It currently sits on the property of Orson Adams, a small distance from its original location."

According to Wikipedia, the first Mormon missionary to visit Georgia was elder John U. Eldredge, who arrived in 1843, thirteen years after Joseph Smith and others founded the Church of Latter-day Saints. "Other missionaries followed to preach and to campaign for Joseph Smith in his presidential bid," Wikipedia explains. After Smith's death in 1844, missionary work in the state stopped until 1878, and the church set up its headquarters for southern missions in Rome, Georgia. "Missionaries were initially treated well upon their return to the South, but before long their success led to violent opposition," notes the Wikipedia entry. "Unable to secure protection for missionaries, the church pulled out all missionaries in Georgia for the next decade. . . . Missionaries returned to Georgia in 1899, but slowly and cautiously due to disease and persecution."

The "violent opposition" included a brutal murder in Whitfield County on July 21, 1879. Twenty-four-year-old Mormon missionary Joseph Standing was traveling with fellow elder Rudger Clawson to a Latter-day Saints church conference in northwest Georgia when a mob approached them near the town of Varnell. Standing was shot twenty times. No one was ever convicted of the crime.

Sadly the Cumorah Church was destroyed by Hurricane Helene in September 2024. These old treasures are fragile, and we are fortunate that we were able to document the church while it was still standing.

According to the *Cumorah Junction* blog, this stage was added in the 1935 renovation. It probably also served as the raised chancel for the pulpit used in church services.

Two classrooms were added to the interior in the 1935 renovation. The classroom on the left also seemed to have a raised floor.

Although many of the windows and doors were missing, the roof seemed relatively new and watertight.

This photo from the Satilla River Saints website shows Joseph Adams, one of south Georgia's earliest Mormon converts, being baptized by "Elder Adam Rufus Brewer, of Utah," in the Satilla River on October 15, 1900. Adams would later donate the land for Cumorah Church. The bankside audience for this event is worth a close look.

Elder Joseph Standing (seated), pictured here with elder Rudger Clawson, was murdered by a mob near the town of Varnell in 1879. His body was taken back to Utah by train, accompanied by Clawson, for a funeral service attended by ten thousand people. A large monument was placed at his grave in 1880.

PHOTOGRAPHY BY GAIL DES JARDIN SEGARS

White Oak Presbyterian

COWETA COUNTY ORG. 1836

According to the church's website, the founders of White Oak were Scots-Irish "Psalm-singing Presbyterians," with roots in Counties Down and Antrim, Ireland. After living in Abbeville, Newberry, and Laurens Districts in South Carolina, they moved to the White Oak community and initially attended worship services at Newnan Presbyterian Church. But after several years, "due to the distance and hardship of traveling, they desired a place of worship closer to their community."

In 1836, these Associate Reformed Presbyterians purchased a log church named Smyrna from the Methodists. The following year, notes the website, the congregation was "solemnly set apart and constituted into a church called White Oak Presbyterian Church." Tradition has it that the organization of the church took place under the shed of the old Bowers cotton gin. The present church was built in 1896.

The cemetery is large, with 523 documented interments, including those of many Civil War veterans. Among them is the Reverend John Hemphill, who is also memorialized with a plaque inside the church. Reverend Hemphill was captured and imprisoned during the war. He subsequently served as pastor of several churches until he was called to White Oak in 1879, serving until his death in 1899. His successor was Ira Sylvester Caldwell, who was serving as pastor when his only child, novelist Erskine Caldwell, was born in 1903.

White Oak Church was built in 1896, and its sanctuary reflects the prosperity of the era.

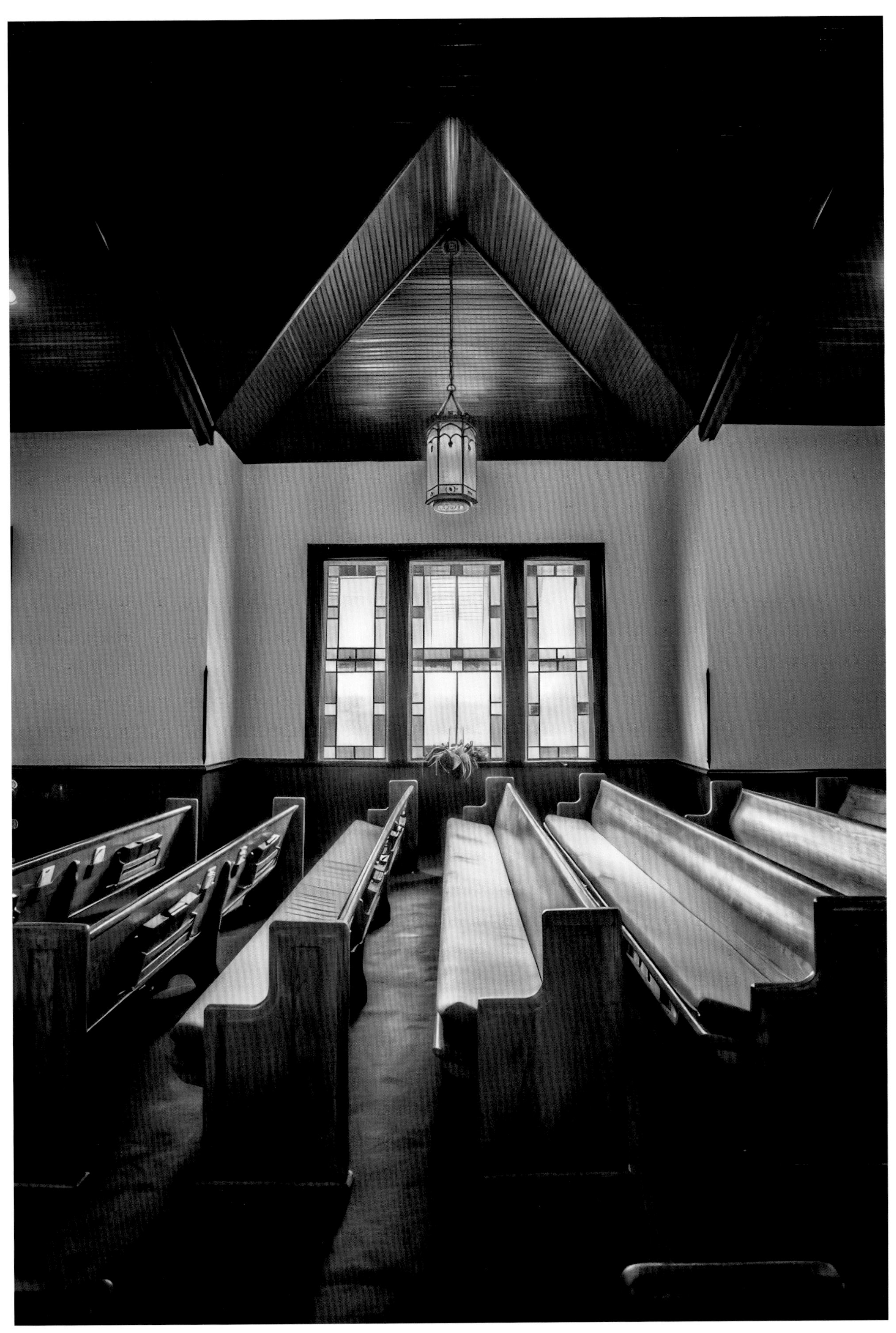

One of the many benefits of the church's cruciform layout is that it allows for the creation of alcoves such as this one, with a suspended truss design. This photograph also shows the stained-glass windowpanes that are present throughout the sanctuary.

Except for the seasonal decorating touches, the chancel, pulpit, apse, and choir area look much as they did in the building's early days, before the turn of the twentieth century.

Authentic, Victorian high-backed chairs sit on either side of the pulpit. Also reflecting the period are the heart pine wainscoting, found throughout the sanctuary, and the maple slat-back chairs for the choir.

A plaque on the sanctuary wall pays tribute to the Reverend John Lind Hemphill, who served as pastor for twenty years in the late 1800s.

The Reverend John Lind Hemphill was born in Abbeville County, South Carolina, on February 21, 1838. A graduate of Erskine College, he volunteered for service at the outbreak of the Civil War and was captured and imprisoned at Elmira, New York. He died unexpectedly on October 30, 1899, and is buried in the cemetery of the church he served for two decades.

PHOTOGRAPHY BY TOM REED

Lumpkin Campground

DAWSON COUNTY ORG. 1830

During the Second Great Awakening of the late eighteenth and early nineteenth centuries, religious fervor spread throughout the United States, particularly in the South. In addition to promoting the growth of Protestant churches, this revivalism popularized the "camp meeting"—a religious gathering held outdoors, full of prayer, preaching, and song. Such meetings were especially prevalent on the frontier, where settlers lacked established houses of worship. Although many of these outdoor meeting spaces have disappeared, some are still in existence, including Lumpkin Campground.

According to its website, the campground was "established in Dawson County in 1830 on 40 acres of land that was purchased when forty men of the Lumpkin County community each donated a dollar." Nearly two centuries later, the original open-air pavilion is still in service. Its red clay floors and carved timbers show the evidence of many generations of use. Over the years, the only modern upgrade to the original arbor has been the addition of electricity.

"In the early days," the website notes, "those who attended camp meetings would come in covered wagons which would also serve as their home for the coming week. Many pulled their cows behind them to furnish milk along with coops of chickens to be killed for meals during the week. They would pack enough ham, eggs, pies and cakes for themselves and enough hay for the animals for a week. In times past when August rolled around and the days stretched out like the long singing of the katydids, it was time to plan for the big gathering of neighbors at Camp Meeting."

Later, the campground saw the addition of rustic cabins, or "tents," around the main pavilion. While the Methodist Church officially owns these tents, some bear the names of families that use them year after year. "Between the tents and the arbor is a large open grove of trees," notes the website, "[whose] trunks are painted with whitewash about four feet from their base. In the time of kerosene lanterns when a family was coming to evening service the dim light would reflect off the painted surface and keep people from bumping into trees." Even today, the trees receive a fresh coat of whitewash before camp meeting begins.

The camp schedule includes singing and preaching twice daily, at eleven o'clock in the morning and seven thirty in the evening. Attendees are called to worship by a conch shell that was brought to the camp from an Alabama beach in 1910.

The rustic but functional tabernacle is designed to accommodate hundreds of worshippers. The open sides with wide eaves allow for maximum cooling air flow while protecting attendees from the rain. The post-and-beam construction kept costs down while providing a stable and sturdy building.

The family "tents" are quite plain and rustic, with no decorative frills. Common bathrooms and showers are available in structures nearby. Though they may appear to be dilapidated, both the older and newer tents provide a functional weeklong home for families, small and large.

Most of the tents are positioned facing the tabernacle, which serves as the "town square." Swings and chairs on each porch furnish space to pass the time between services and to visit with passersby.

The paint on the trees provides insect control as well as nighttime visibility.

Some of the oldest "tents" are a bit more primitive than the newer ones, with amenities and furniture in the hands of the people who use them year after year. Still, all have a porch area and provide the closeness of contact within the family and with other attendees.

This photo captures the authenticity and atmosphere that permeate the camp meeting, creating the ambience that has attracted worshippers for almost two hundred years. Except for lights and ceiling fans, these attendees are enjoying an experience similar to that of their forebears back in the beginning.

PHOTOGRAPHY BY BRYAN STOVALL

Mizpah Methodist

EFFINGHAM COUNTY ORG. 1859

The church's history begins in 1858, when Dr. Anderson P. Longstreet, a young physician and surgeon, and his family moved from Rome, Georgia, to what was to become the Mizpah community in Effingham County. His wife, Laura Ayer Longstreet, came from a family of staunch Methodists in South Carolina, where they had previously started several churches. According to church records, Laura's father, Dr. Cornelius K. Ayer, provided the initial donation for Mizpah Methodist, and ultimately the congregation raised a total of $632. L. S. Malone was selected as the builder for a structure that would measure 35 by 50 by 13 feet. Four acres of land for the church and a cemetery were purchased from George Best for twelve dollars. The members themselves donated lumber, materials, and much of the labor. On Sunday, December 18, 1859, Mizpah held its first worship service with twenty male and twenty female members.

Over the years, improvements and additions have been made, but the original structure and supports are still intact. The church originally had two entrances, one for men and one for women and children. The center aisle had a partition down the middle to enforce this separation, which was quite common in rural churches of the era. Later, in 1886, one double door entrance and an undivided center aisle replaced the original layout. A porch was added at that time.

Rural churches were the center of the community and took an active role in disciplining members who were engaged in one form of sin or another. Those who were accused of wrongdoing would be brought before a committee and given a chance for redemption. Repeated offenses or lack of sufficient repentance could result in expulsion from the church. For instance, church records show that in 1893 a church member was accused of dancing, considered a very serious offense at that time. Fortunately, the guilty party confessed to the pastor and received forgiveness.

Today, Mizpah has an active congregation and remains at its original location, surrounded by lush pine forests and cultivated fields. Many of Effingham County's early settlers are buried in the cemetery, and descendants of some of the original members, such as the Porters, sit in the pews. Mizpah Methodist is the home church of the current speaker of the Georgia House of Representatives, Jon G. Burns Sr., and his family.

Although Mizpah has seen many improvements over the years, the basic structure is intact. The church originally had two entrances, as well as partitioned pews in the center, to separate men from women and children. In 1886 the layout changed to have a single entrance and a center aisle.

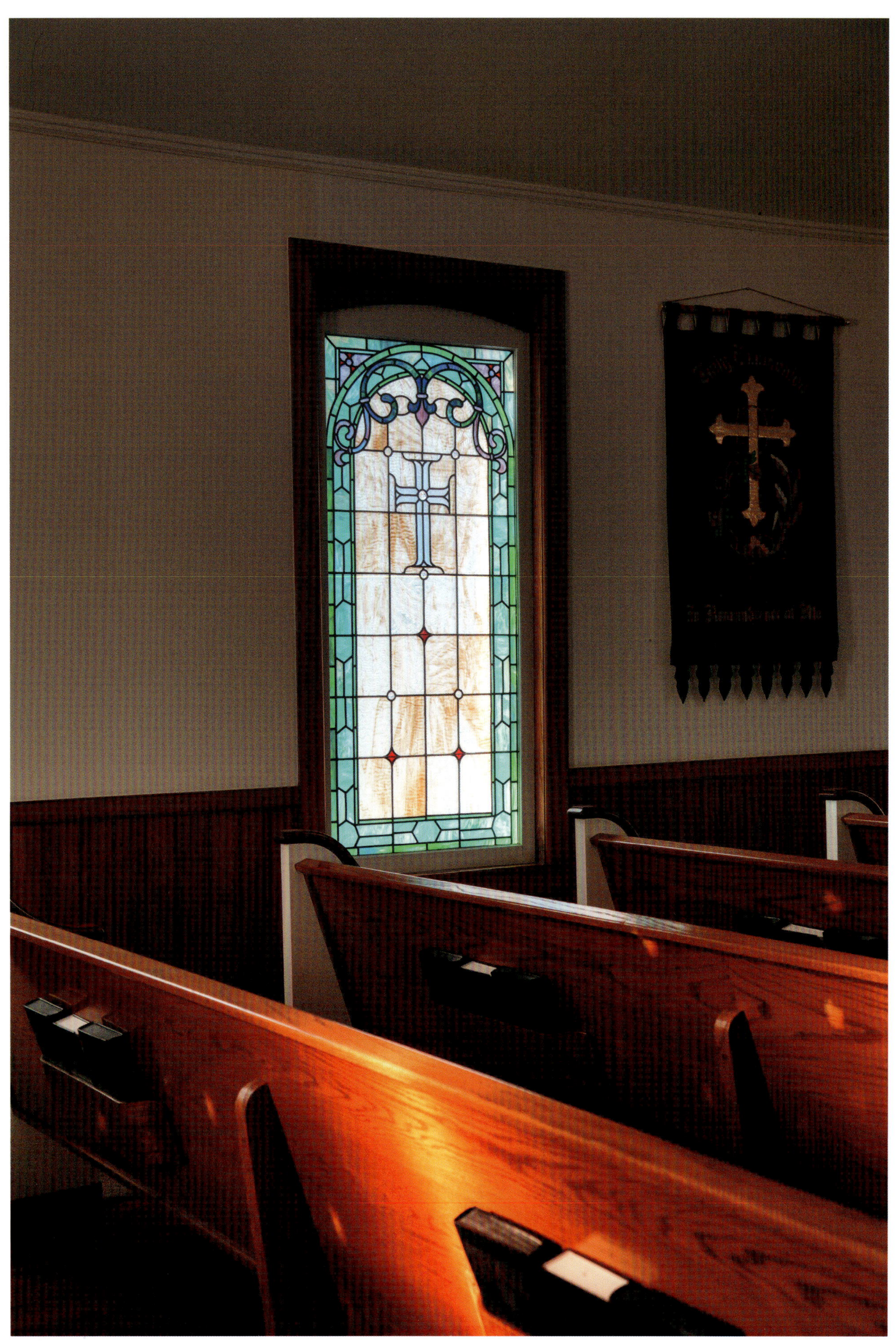

The heart pine wainscoting and matching floors reflect the natural materials that are so common in this part of Georgia. The stained-glass windows were added later.

This well-used Bible is a relic of Mizpah's past.

Here lie Edward Benning Porter and his wife, Margaret. According to Find a Grave, Margaret was born in Beaufort County, South Carolina, in 1836. She and Edward had eleven children. The Porter roots run deep in this part of Georgia. Of the 243 recorded graves at Mizpah, thirty-one have the surname Porter.

PHOTOGRAPHY BY RANDY CLEGG

Ruckersville Methodist

ELBERT COUNTY ORG. 1796

The little white church pictured here is near the Savannah River in what was once the village of Ruckersville, one of the earliest European settlements in Georgia. The church was organized in 1796 but moved to its present site in 1832 when Peter Alexander donated 3 acres of land for construction of the current building, which was completed the following year. Eighteen members of the Alexander family are buried in the cemetery.

The churchyard also contains the headstone of Paul Gaines, who fell ill and died in late 1899 at the age of sixteen while doing military service in what became known as the Philippine Insurrection. Private Gaines's body was sent home via a steamship, arriving on the U.S. mainland on February 24, 1900. The *San Francisco Chronicle* proclaimed, "Steamship Hancock Arrives from Manilla . . . She Has on Board the Bodies of Five Hundred Soldiers Who Fell in the Philippines—An Eventful Voyage."

Ruckersville Methodist continues to be an active church. Its sanctuary has been altered over the years, most significantly in 1959, when the pews were replaced with seats from a theater in Augusta. Recent work has focused on returning several interior features to their original 1833 appearance.

Although few signs of it exist today, Ruckersville was once a bustling community. The Find a Grave website notes that it received its name from Joseph Rucker (1788–1864), whose family moved from Orange County, Virginia, in 1788 and amassed a large amount of land in eighteenth-century Georgia. Joseph made his home on the headwaters of Van's Creek and named the growing village Ruckersville, in tribute to the Virginia hometown of his father. At one time, Joseph was the owner of twelve plantations and was referred to as Squire Rucker. He was also considered Georgia's first millionaire.

According to a September 19, 1929, article in the *Elberton (Georgia) Star*, Ruckersville "once . . . had fifty stores, two banks and a newspaper." Moreover, "it was the depot for distribution of freight for all points above Petersburg, the freight being brought up the Savannah river by pole boats. It had two schools, and an academy of which a Princeton graduate was principal."

Today little remains of the town, other than a few cemeteries and the Methodist church.

This view from the central entrance shows the old woodwork and the raised chancel. Both have been recently refurbished.

The Ruckersville cemetery predates the present church by several years. There are 171 recorded interments, the oldest being that of William Alston, who died in 1810. One of many veterans laid to rest in the cemetery, he was a member of the North Carolina Provincial Congress in 1775 and served as a lieutenant colonel in the Revolutionary War.

At one time, Joseph Rucker (1788–1864) owned as many as twelve plantations. He was said to be Georgia's first millionaire, and he was known as Squire Rucker. The Civil War devastated all of his plantations, including Cedar Grove, where he made his home.

This headstone memorializes Paul Gaines, a sixteen-year-old soldier from Company L of the Twenty-Ninth Infantry, United States Volunteers. He died of peritonitis in Manila in December 1899 at the beginning of what became known as the Philippine Insurrection.

PHOTOGRAPHY BY TOM REED

Tarpley Chapel

FANNIN COUNTY ORG. 1890

This church, in rural Fannin County, began its existence as Pleasant Gap Methodist. At some point it was renamed in honor of its founders, the Tarpley family, whose descendants are still active in its maintenance. The history of the family is richly documented in the book *Facets of Fannin: A History of Fannin County, Georgia*, which was one of our primary sources of information. We also drew from a family history furnished by Nellie Abercrombie and from articles in the *Blue Ridge Summit-Post*, as well as from the Find a Grave website.

Originally from England, the Tarpleys migrated to North America prior to 1664, where they made a living as tobacco farmers. According to Find a Grave, family members ultimately made their way to Georgia when Mason Tarpley (1820–1907), his older brother James Allen Tarpley (1818–1909), and their wives—both of whom were named Sarah—moved to what is now Fannin County in 1850. Mason acquired a large plot of land beside the Toccoa River, where he and Sarah farmed and raised their family of six boys and two girls. In addition to farming, Mason was a Methodist Circuit preacher who pastored several congregations in Fannin County.

One of James Allen's sons was Linzy Tarpley, who married Martha Ware in 1872. Linzy and Martha raised a family of eight children on their farm. In 1890 James deeded land to his son to build a church. The church was made of logs and had a dirt floor. In 1908 the decision was made to build a larger and more comfortable church, and the new church was dedicated in June 1911.

The Tarpley family typifies how the north Georgia mountains were settled after the Cherokees were expelled, as a result of the Indian Removal Act of 1830. Their family roots have been in this part of Georgia now for almost two hundred years. James Allen and Sarah are buried in the graveyard, as is their son Linzy. Little Sadie Tarpley, shown in the photo when she was two, is also there, having died at the age of eight.

Tarpley Chapel is a remarkably well-preserved example of a 120-year-old rural mountain church. The church is a tribute to the Tarpley family and their respect for their heritage.

Most of the original window frames and panes are still in place. The pews are original—very simple in construction and not built for comfort.

The walls and ceiling are of wood planking. Because the building has been well cared for, there is no evidence of the water damage to ceilings, windows, walls, and floors that is so common in older churches.

The graveyard is small, with only twenty-one graves. In the foreground is the headstone of Linzy Green Tarpley (1849–1916). His father, James Allen Tarpley (1818–1909), is buried beneath the third headstone.

James Allen Tarpley was born May 10, 1818, in Halifax County, Virginia, and married Sarah Vann Austin on November 16, 1840, in Caswell County, North Carolina. He moved to what is now Fannin County, Georgia, around 1850.

This 1913 photo shows Linzy Tarpley with his wife, Martha, and two of their granddaughters, Ora Jane and Sadie. It illustrates the difficulty of carving out a life in the north Georgia mountains. Sadie died in February 1920, at the age of eight.

PHOTOGRAPHY BY TOM REED

Chubb Chapel Methodist

FLOYD COUNTY ORG. 1870

Chubb Chapel Methodist, built in 1870, is one of the older African American churches in rural Georgia. This Gothic Revival structure is unusual in both its architecture and its history, as it is the last surviving structure of Chubbtown, one of Georgia's few communities established by free Black people prior to emancipation.

According to the National Register of Historic Places, the Chubb family—which founded the town that bears its name—can trace its roots in North America as far back as 1775. Isaac Chubb, born about 1797 in North Carolina, appeared as a free Black man in the 1830 census of Caswell County, North Carolina. He migrated to Georgia sometime before 1833. His first child is recorded as having been born in Georgia that year. The 1850 census shows the Isaac Chubb family was domiciled in Morgan County, Georgia. In the early 1860s, the family moved to their new home in northwest Georgia.

Isaac had eight sons, and those Chubb brothers began purchasing real estate as early as 1864. In time, these holdings became home to a self-sufficient community, which provided goods and services to white and Black residents of the surrounding areas. The community, serviced by its own post office, was composed of a general store, blacksmith shop, gristmill, distillery, syrup mill, sawmill, wagon company, cotton gin, and casket factory. The 1870 census lists the various Chubb brothers as blacksmiths, wagonmakers, house carpenters, sawmill operators, and farmers.

On August 8, 1870, Henry Chubb and his brothers sold one acre of land for $200 to the trustees of the Methodist Episcopal Church. Chubb Chapel was built later that year. It was added to the National Register of Historic Places in 1990 and continues to serve as a church in the United Methodist denomination.

Some Chubb family members still live in the area as well as in nearby Cave Spring, Cedartown, and Rome. Others have migrated to places across the United States. Today, Chubb descendants work in the fields of ministry, education, law, medicine, insurance, and construction, as well as in corporations and the service industries. Among the best known family members are Nick and Bradley Chubb, who played for the University of Georgia and North Carolina State football teams, respectively, before going on to play in the National Football League.

This view from the pulpit reveals the simplicity of design and decoration within this Gothic Revival sanctuary. In the rear are the two traditional entry doors, one for men and the other for women and children, even though that practice was beginning to fade when this church was built. The traditional chancel, bordered by a balustrade, incorporates the step up into the altar, pulpit, and apse area.

Though many changes have occurred in the sanctuary, the design and decoration remain much as they were in 1870. The original 14-foot-high, board-and-batten heart pine ceiling mirrors the exterior treatment at Chubb and is still in place. Also intact are the heart pine horizontal wallboards, doors, and stout support columns. The original tall, clear-glass windows still allow the church to fill with natural light on sunny days.

PHOTOGRAPHY BY GAIL DES JARDIN SEGARS

Glendale Chapel Methodist

FLOYD COUNTY ORG. 1875

Glendale Chapel Methodist Church, located in the foothills of northwest Georgia, stands today because a community came together to save it from a fate that has befallen so many rural churches. We frequently see their disintegrating remains on Georgia backroads.

In the early days after its founding in 1875, members of Glendale Methodist worshipped in a brush arbor near its current location and then in a log structure on the same property. The congregation moved into the little chapel pictured here in 1889.

Over the years, the chapel also served as a school—the only source of education for Black children in this remote part of northwest Georgia. Eventually, Georgia's rural attrition took its toll, and the last known gathering in the chapel took place in 1988. The building fell into disrepair and might have disappeared completely if not for the efforts of five women who were determined to preserve it.

Annie Shields and Patricia York were equestrian therapists who owned property adjacent to the Glendale church. While looking for more space in which to exercise their horses they stumbled upon the chapel's ruins and became interested in restoring it. They joined forces with three former congregants—Annie M. Johnson, Jennie Johnson Jones, and Alva Johnson Battey—who were great-granddaughters of church founders Green and Rachel Johnson. They, too, wished to preserve this important piece of Georgia history.

As the restoration began, the forces of time, weather, and neglect fought back, and the old building literally fell apart. No one was hurt, and the preservationists were undeterred. After discovering the original church had been unpainted and was constructed in the board-and-batten style from white oak trees cut from the property, they decided to go forward with the original construction style and salvage as much material from the ruins as they could.

The results were documented in before-and-after pictures that provide a glimpse into the lives of those who worshipped and studied in this little chapel in the deep woods of Floyd County.

We are looking at a pre-restoration 2015 photograph of a very dilapidated Glendale Chapel. It shows the state of disrepair this old church was in at that time.

This close-up view of the chapel, taken in 2015, gives some sense of the scale of the renovation project. During the early demolition phase, the walls collapsed, but the decision was made to continue and salvage as much of the original material as possible.

In this more recent photo of the finished sanctuary, the eight pews—exact replicas of the originals in size and design—sit on vintage floorboards salvaged from original materials. The interior horizontal wallboards and vertical thin ceiling boards are painted light green. The trussed rafter ceiling rises to create a cathedral-like atmosphere.

This close-up view reveals the simple but elegant chancel and pulpit. The pulpit had gone missing for over forty years before it was rediscovered, repaired, and then returned to its place at Glendale Chapel.

In keeping with the desire to create an authentic atmosphere at the chapel, the sanctuary is heated by an old-fashioned wood-burning stove.

PHOTOGRAPHY BY SAM RATCLIFFE

Possum Trot Church

FLOYD COUNTY ORG. 1850S

The exact date of the organization and construction of Possum Trot Church is unknown, but it is believed to date from the 1850s. By the late 1800s, the church had been abandoned. However, in 1900, it was repurposed as a Sunday school for the Possum Trot community by Martha Berry, the daughter of a wealthy Floyd County planter. Martha devoted the rest of her life to education in her northwest Georgia community, and she founded several schools, including the one that would bear her name—Berry College in Rome.

Martha McChesney Berry was born on October 7, 1865, in Alabama, to Frances Margaret Rhea and Thomas Berry. Her Scots-Irish ancestors came to the British colonies in North America in the first half of the eighteenth century. Her mother was the daughter of an Alabama planter. Her father was a lieutenant in the Mexican-American War, a forty-niner in the California gold rush, and a captain for the Confederacy in the Civil War. The family moved to Rome, Georgia, when she was still a baby, and she lived there for the rest of her life.

At the turn of the century, rural people in this part of northwest Georgia had very limited access to traditional education or to what we know today as Sunday school. Martha was determined to help fill this void, and because of her work, she became known as the "Sunday Lady of Possum Trot." The Possum Trot Sunday school had a modest beginning but by 1902, whole families filled the small church.

Because there were not enough Bibles for all students to use, verses were painted on the chapel walls. In the early 1930s, schoolrooms were added at the church location, and formal grammar school education was offered. During World War II, and for a short period following, the Possum Trot school was closed. It reopened in 1948 but closed again in 1954.

The students at Berry College, as well as alumni volunteers, have worked on restoring the old complex. Berry College's website is the source for the above information.

This is the view that greets visitors upon entering Possum Trot Church. The dark-stained wood surfaces take on a warm glow when bathed in light from the clear-glass nine-over-nine windows.

BUT JESUS SAID,
SUFFER LITT CHILDREN TO
COME UNTO ME, ORBID THEM NOT
FOR OF SUCH IS KINGDOM OF GOD.
THIS IS A FAITHFUL SAYING,
AND WORTHY OF ALL ACCEPTATION,
THAT CHRIST JESUS CAME INTO THE
WORLD TO SAVE SINNERS.
FOR GOD SO LOVED TH LD, THAT
HE GAVE HIS ONLY BEGO ON, THAT
WHOSOEVER BELIEVETH IN OULD NOT
PERISH, BUT HAVE EVERLA LIFE.

Martha Berry felt it was proper for all students to be constantly exposed to Scripture. The "amen corner" features one of the many quotes from the Bible that adorn most of the interior walls.

The interior of Possum Trot features narrow, horizontal wallboards, many of which are inscribed with Scripture.

PHOTOGRAPHY BY TOM REED

Ridgeway Baptist

GILMER COUNTY ORG. 1865

It is unclear when the congregation of Ridgeway Baptist—originally called New Bethel—was formed, but according to Greg McClure's *History of Ridgeway Baptist Church*, the building itself was constructed in 1865 by Confederate veterans J. W. Pankey, J. C. Worley, Frank Nelson, and Leander Corbin after they returned from the war. The old log church was a one-room structure with a dirt floor, two doors, and three windows with shutters. A plank floor was added at some point. Other improvements included an extension, built in 1940, and electricity, which was not installed until 1949. A new church was built across the street in 1982.

Early rural churches were built of local materials and reflected what the community could afford. Normally churches would evolve from a brush arbor, to a log church, and finally to a framed sanctuary. Many church records in Georgia reflect this progression, but very few of these early log churches have survived. This is one of them. It reflects the difficult economic circumstances these rugged mountain people faced in the nineteenth century. In the graveyard, meanwhile, lie tales of the Civil War, moonshiners, and murder.

This was not plantation country, and growing cotton was not an option. However, there was another "cash crop"—homemade liquor. Unsurprisingly, the U.S. government's decision to tax all whiskey sales and then to enforce this mandate with federal agents in the years following the Civil War caused much conflict in northwest Georgia—which brings us to the Ridgeway cemetery and the story of Henry Worley.

In the late 1800s and early 1900s, Gilmer County, like several other areas of the United States, was home to a self-styled band of vigilantes known as the Whitecaps, a secret society that began in Indiana in the 1830s. Their purpose was to enforce their own moral code, which, in northwest Georgia, included support for making moonshine. When local resident Henry Worley was suspected of passing along information about liquor sales to the despised federal revenue agents, a large group of Whitecaps came to his home, took him a few miles away, and tried to hang him. Incredibly, he was able to escape and made his way back to his home in the Ridgeway community.

Sometime later, a smaller number of Whitecaps returned and gunned Worley down in his cornfield, in front of his daughter, Kemmie. Several Whitecaps were indicted for the crime, but ultimately only two, John Quarles Sr. and David Butler, were sent to prison, both with five-year sentences. The judge reportedly reduced the original ten-year sentences because of the poverty of the defendants and the fact that Quarles had fourteen children and Butler had eight. Quarles, however, died while incarcerated in Columbus, Ohio, and is buried there.

The Atlanta papers covering the trial were full of front-page tales of plain mountain folks being terrorized by this gang of Whitecap vigilantes, whose power was now broken. In the graveyard, Henry Worley's daughter, Kemmie, is buried a few feet from her parents alongside her husband, Henry Quarles—-the nephew of the man who was convicted of her father's murder.

This log cabin was built in 1865 by Gilmer County men who were returning home after the Civil War. The fact that Ridgeway still stands is remarkable.

Music and singing have always been an integral part of Baptist worship. This nineteenth-century upright piano was probably bought in Dahlonega, Chattanooga, or another nearby city. It would have been a costly but essential purchase.

The exposed column next to the large, crude exit door is evidence of the church's 1940 expansion, which provided a larger pulpit area for the sanctuary. The simple pulpit, bench, and pews in the "amen corner" are authentic relics of earlier church history.

The main entry door, like the rest of the interior at Ridgeway, is prosaic and was probably store-bought to replace one that had worn out over time. The pews feature scrolled end caps and pieced backs—among the few decorative elements in this old sanctuary.

The Ridgeway cemetery contains 172 documented interments, including twenty-nine associated with the Quarles family and sixteen with the surname Pankey. The grave in the foreground is that of James W. Pankey, one of the returning Confederates who built the log church in 1865.

Henry Worley was laid to rest in the Ridgeway cemetery the day after he was murdered in his cornfield. Next to him lie his daughter, Kemmie, who was with him the day he died, and her husband, Henry B. Quarles, whose uncle was sent to a Columbus, Ohio, prison for killing Worley.

PHOTOGRAPHY BY BRYAN STOVALL

Good Shepherd Episcopal

GLYNN COUNTY ORG. 1894

The photo here shows Good Shepherd Episcopal Church, built in 1928, and the parochial school next door, built in 1901. Both were founded by Anna Alexander, who was consecrated as an Episcopal Church deaconess in 1907—the only African American ever to receive that designation. Her story is one of dedication, service, and determination to serve her coastal community of Pennick, located near St. Simons Island.

In the early 1900s, the schoolhouse served as both school and church as well as living quarters for Alexander. It is one of only a handful of African American church-sponsored school structures left in Georgia. The school has long been closed, but the church is still active. Our primary source of information about Good Shepherd and the woman who founded it was an in-depth article from the *Brunswick News* published on October 31, 2015.

Alexander was born in 1865 to parents who had been enslaved on the infamous Butler Island Plantation, across the river from Darien. Her mother, Daphne, was the biracial daughter of white plantation manager Roswell King Jr., who later founded the town of Roswell. Her father, James, was one of the few slaves who had been allowed to receive some education, and he became the personal assistant of plantation owner Pierce Butler. Daphne and James Alexander had eleven children, many of whom became active in the Darien community and especially at St. Cyprian's Episcopal Church.

Anna, raised in the Episcopal Church, found the Glynn County public education available to her was substandard. She became a teacher at the parochial school attached to St. Cyprian's that her sister, Mary Alexander Mann, had founded. In 1894 she prompted the founding of an Episcopal mission, the Church of the Good Shepherd, in the community of Pennick, and subsequently established the school. Like St. Cyprian's, the one-room Good

Shepherd school provided virtually the only access to adequate education for local African American children in the years following the Civil War.

In 1998, Anna was named a saint of Georgia by the Diocese of Georgia, affirming the deep impact she and her school had on her community. The Good Shepherd school was included in the 2022 "Places in Peril" list by the Georgia Trust for Historic Preservation.

The ceiling and roof architectural elements provide a decorative, cathedral-like atmosphere in the sanctuary.

This photo reflects the warm glow of the heart pine floors, the walls, and the handmade plane marks visible on the original pews. Very large trees must have been used to yield the wide, single-plank construction.

Rather than the Gothic windows that were common in the early twentieth century, the windows and frames at Good Shepherd are all in the Roman style, with large panes set into contrasting frames. The narrow, horizontal tongue-and-groove walls above the wainscoting and contrasting chair rail also add to the beauty of the sanctuary.

This view of the school looks toward a step-up chancel and door. In the back is a foot pump organ, and on the left is a piano in front of the original chalkboard. The rear door may have opened onto a stair leading up to Anna's tiny living quarters on the second floor.

Deaconess Alexander died September 24, 1947, and is buried in front of the school that also served as her home.

Here is a rare photo of Deaconess Alexander with her students. Working with children of diverse ages was one of the challenges faced by teachers in one-room schools.

PHOTOGRAPHY BY WAYNE MOORE

Needwood Baptist

GLYNN COUNTY ORG. 1866

Needwood Baptist Church, originally named Broadfield, was organized in 1866 by former slaves from nearby plantations. It was first on land belonging to the Hofwyl-Broadfield Plantation, now a state-owned historical site located one mile away. Sometime in the 1880s it was moved to the present location and its name changed from Broadfield to Needwood. It is believed that the original structure was built in the 1870s, according to the National Register of Historic Places, to which it was added in 1998.

Architecturally, the church is representative of many African American places of worship constructed in the decades following the Civil War—simple and lacking in ornate ornamentation. On the inside, wooden tongue-and-groove boards compose the walls and the ceiling. The pews are original. The National Register notes that the frame itself was constructed in the "modified post and beam/balloon" style, which was popular in the 1870s. A bell in one of the towers is believed to have been cast in 1884 in Baltimore and is perhaps the most significant treasure in the church.

On the same plot of land sits a one-room schoolhouse, believed to have been constructed prior to 1907. Although many such schools were built in the post–Civil War South to serve African American children, Needwood is one of the very few that survive today. Generations of Black students from the area received their first- through sixth-grade education at Needwood School. Those who continued their studies into the seventh grade attended Risley Elementary in Brunswick. In the 1940s and 1950s, that meant buying commuter tickets for the Greyhound bus line, since Black children were not allowed to ride on school buses.

According to the National Register, Needwood Church did not own the school property until 1954. It continued to serve as a school into the 1950s or 1960s, at which time court-ordered integration made public education widely available to Black students.

Above the piano at the cased opening, clear signs of roof leaks can be seen. Water damage is also evident around the ceiling globe light. On the other hand, the neat and attractive raised chancel area provides evidence that the building is being maintained, even though it is used only for special occasions.

Almost everything in this photo is original. The National Register of Historic Places describes the interior as "wood-tongue-and-groove board [on] both ceilings and walls," adding, "The wall boards are mounted horizontally, except for a wainscot of vertical boarding, approximately three feet high."

Needwood's interior, though showing wear commensurate with its nearly 150 years of age, remains in fair to good condition. The sanctuary contains many old furnishings, including the pastor's chair, the pulpit, a table, a baptism set, a chalice, and even a spittoon. The dark pine pews are said to be the originals.

The National Register of Historic Places notes that Needwood's lumber is "a mixture of hand-hewn timbers and milled material." In the ceiling, the "joists which span the width of the structure are hand-hewn timbers, while the rafters are mill-sawn lumber. Cut nails are used throughout the structure."

Little one-room schools such as this were scattered all over Georgia in the early 1900s. Not many are left. This one served the Needwood community for more than fifty years.

PHOTOGRAPHY BY SCOTT FARRAR

Siloam Presbyterian

GREENE COUNTY ORG. 1903

According to church records, Siloam Presbyterian had its origins in Hastings Church, which local resident John T. Dolvin (1827–1910) organized in 1894–95. A few years after its founding, members decided to move the church a few miles southeast to the community of Siloam. They dismantled Hastings Church and used the materials to construct a new building on land donated by the local Baptist church, which was across the street. Completed by the spring of 1903, the new church was named Siloam Presbyterian.

The church nearly burned down on March 31, 1929, when one of the members, a Mrs. Rhodes, arrived early to bring flowers and make a fire in the new heater. She accidentally used the gasoline container, and an explosion occurred as she lit the fire. Frantically, she fought the flames with her clothes and bare hands in an effort to save the church—and she did, at the cost of her life. After several weeks of agony, she died from her injuries.

Siloam has not always been the nearly deserted town that it is today. In a memoir called *Two Years to Remember*, renowned rural sociologist Arthur Raper and his daughter, Martha, describe the bustling social life of the town in the 1930s and 1940s. The book includes anecdotes about Saturday trips to the general store and Sunday trips to Siloam Presbyterian. During his residence in Greene County, Arthur Raper also wrote *Sharecroppers All* and *Tenants of the Almighty*, both of which focused on Southern farmworkers during the Depression.

This view has not changed much in the last 120 years. A pulpit Bible that Dr. and Mrs. C. F. Durham presented to the Hastings Church in 1895 is still in use today.

When John Dolvin and his fellow congregants walked into the new Siloam Presbyterian sanctuary in 1903, they must have felt a sense of homecoming as they settled into the original pews brought over from Hastings Church.

Though it is no longer functioning, an old pump organ remains in the sanctuary, to the right of the chancel.

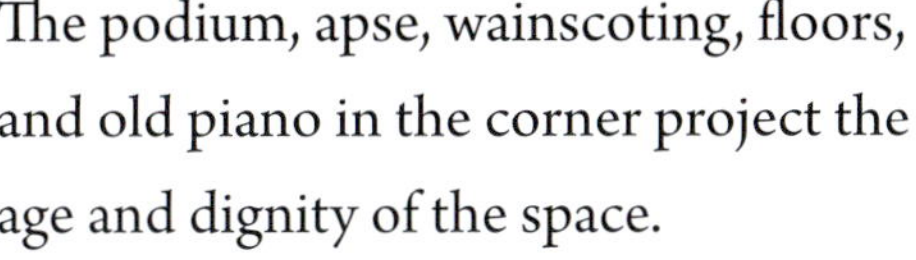

The podium, apse, wainscoting, floors, and old piano in the corner project the age and dignity of the space.

Among those buried at Siloam Cemetery are Jennie Williams (July 7, 1844–October 3, 1898) and her husband, Harrison O'Neal (January 19, 1839–May 27, 1921). According to Find a Grave, Harrison enlisted in the Confederate army in May 1862 and was wounded at the Battle of Gettysburg the following year. He rejoined his unit and remained until the final surrender at Appomattox. The couple had at least one child, Charles O'Neal, who was listed as age seven in the 1880 census.

PHOTOGRAPHY BY RANDY CLEGG

Mount Airy Presbyterian

HABERSHAM COUNTY ORG. 1906

Mount Airy Presbyterian was organized with ten charter members in 1906, and the structure was completed in 1907. Its architecture reflects its early twentieth-century Presbyterian heritage—simple yet elegant. At the time, the town of Mount Airy was a prominent resort destination that had a well-known hotel called the Monterey. During the summer months, it attracted many visitors from Atlanta and the coastal areas of Georgia and South Carolina. Dr. S. L. Morris, a Presbyterian minister and secretary of the denomination's home mission board, had a summer home in Mount Airy and was instrumental in founding the church. Dr. Henry F. Hoyt, pastor of nearby Cornelia Presbyterian, assisted at the organizational meeting of the Mount Airy Church.

Dr. Morris reported to the presbytery that the building's construction cost was $1,000, with an additional expense of $250 for the pews. Although it was always a small church with never more than about twenty-five members, the church played an important role in the life of the village, attracting children from other churches to its Sunday school, donating food and clothing for the needy, and sponsoring an annual community Christmas party. By 1979, its members had become so few that it merged with Cornelia Presbyterian. The building, which is now a chapel of the Cornelia church, remains unchanged and contains its original furnishings.

Georgia is dotted with Presbyterian churches that were built in the late nineteenth and early twentieth centuries, a period of optimism and relatively good financial health in most of the state. The fact that Mount Airy was founded primarily to serve families at their summer homes is evidence of this prosperity.

The somewhat austere sanctuary reflects the Presbyterian tendency to avoid ostentation and highly decorative houses of worship. On the other hand, the quality of the construction materials, the plaster walls, the beadboard ceiling, the handsomely designed and finished pews, the striking chandelier, and the Gothic windows reflect the congregation's sense of pride and good taste.

Perhaps the most obvious indications of the founding congregation's wealth are the high-quality furnishings in the sanctuary. These include the pews, communion table, silver service and baptismal, elaborate chairs, and pump organ.

This photo, taken from behind the pulpit, includes a panoramic view of the north Georgia countryside as seen through the Gothic windows.

Here is a closer look at the original heart pine floors, beadboard wainscoting, and chair rail. The piano, a recent gift to Mount Airy Chapel, is a rare square grand, a relic of the nineteenth century. It could be older than the building itself.

This eclectic, unusually styled chair and its twin have been used at the chapel continuously for over a century. The chapel's Gothic windows are cleverly designed, allowing the lower sash to be raised even though the upper sash consists of a pointed arch.

PHOTOGRAPHY BY SCOTT FARRAR

Mount Zion Presbyterian

HANCOCK COUNTY ORG. 1813

Mount Zion Presbyterian, sited on a high piece of ground with a commanding view of the countryside, is visible from the highway. Designed in the Greek Revival style, it has four large columns supporting an elevated portico, with double-door entrances leading to an interesting double-aisle pew arrangement. Originally founded as a Presbyterian church, it was sold to the trustees of a Methodist church in 1903 and became inactive in 1958.

The community of Mount Zion has a storied history as an education center, developed under the leadership of the Reverend Nathan Beman. Reverend Beman was a learned man who moved from Maine to Georgia in 1812. Shortly thereafter, he agreed to serve as the headmaster of the academy at Mount Zion, as well as pastor of the Mount Zion Presbyterian Church. Although the school was established before his arrival in the area, it was Beman's leadership that turned it into one of Georgia's most celebrated academic institutions. Its graduates included William J. Northen, who served as governor of Georgia from 1890 to 1894, as well as famous educators and writers.

At one time, the village consisted of the church, a two-story school, many houses, and various other buildings. But over time, nearly all traces of it have entirely vanished, leaving the church as the only remaining building in this once-prosperous center of learning. Built in 1814, this is the original structure—which is unusual, since most churches in the rural backcountry started as brush arbors, then progressed to log churches, and finally to one or more versions of a framed sanctuary. The building is currently owned by the Hancock County Historical Society and is open to respectful visitors.

Many of Hancock County's earliest white settlers are buried in the church graveyard. There are seventy-three recorded interments with headstones, but others are surely there in unmarked graves. Many old cemeteries contain more unmarked graves than marked—usually due to the use of wooden markers or small fieldstones that disappear over time.

The foundation of Mount Zion Presbyterian Church rests on unmortared and irregular stacks of fieldstones. The difference in height reflects the back-to-front grade of the property. Amazingly, this form of construction yielded a church that is completely level after two hundred years.

The unusual, imposing structure of the three-step chancel contrasts with the simple pew design and creates an ambience of authority.

The sanctuary features a double-aisle arrangement of pews, along with high twelve-over-twelve windows and wide Georgia pine floors. There are two front entrances off the large porch—one for men and another for women and children—and the center pews are also divided by gender.

Unlike most churches in the rural backcountry, which started in brush arbors before moving into a log building and then a framed structure, Mount Zion constructed its building soon after it was organized as a congregation. According to the Forgotten South website, church members raised $700 for the structure—a sum that reflected the wealth of the congregation.

This tombstone in the Mount Zion cemetery reads, “To the memory of a departed child—She was lovely in life and peaceful in death.” Although the name on the stone is spelled Josee Siuvers (July 23, 1833–July 27, 1853), other records identify this young woman as Josephine “Josie” Shivers, daughter of Barnaby Shivers (1775–1851) and Sarah Little (1804–81). The 1850 Hancock County census lists Josephine Shivers, age seventeen, in the household of Barnaby Shivers, age seventy-five, and Sarah H. Shivers, age forty-five.

The high twelve-over-twelve windows built over the wide, horizontal wainscoting and chair rail allow a great deal of light into the sanctuary. The white pews and the natural pine floors blend in with the painted walls. The double aisle arrangement required that there be a row of short pews on either side that butt into the wainscoting.

PHOTOGRAPHY BY SCOTT FARRAR

Rock Mills Methodist

HANCOCK COUNTY ORG. 1840

The original benefactor of Rock Mills Methodist—later known as Jewell Methodist—was William Shivers, who was born in 1783 in Edgecombe County, North Carolina. According to the National Register of Historic Places, he was the son of Jonas Shivers, a Revolutionary War soldier who settled in Hancock County sometime before 1810. By 1820, the younger Shivers owned Rock Mill Plantation, which consisted of a large house, a gristmill, a cotton carding mill, and support buildings.

In 1840, William donated 3 acres of land to establish a Methodist church. A document titled "History of the Methodist Church, Jewell, Georgia" noted that the church's original location was "just off the Jewell-Mayfield Road," about a mile and a quarter from Jewell. Rock Mills Methodist remained on these 3 acres until 1894, when it was moved to the Jewell community, across the street from the Jewell Baptist Church. According to the church history, the land for the new location was given by Dr. J. W. Rhodes (1847–1909), who is buried at the Baptist church cemetery.

Many revivals were held at the church, most notably in 1868, when forty new members joined. Bishops George F. Pierce (1811–84) and Lucius Holsey (1842–1920), an African American, preached at Rock Mills Methodist. By 1877, a Sunday school was organized and the congregation purchased its first organ, despite the protests of older, more traditional members. In 1881, the Woman's Missionary Society was established.

The town of Jewell is named for Daniel Ashley Jewell (1822–96), who migrated from New Hampshire in the 1840s and established Jewell Cotton Mills, on the nearby Ogeechee River shoals. In 1870, he founded the church across the street, which became

Jewell Baptist. It is made of handmade bricks and designed to be a replica of the church in Winchester, New Hampshire, where Mr. Jewell was raised.

In 1927, when the Jewell Mills burned, many families moved away, and membership dwindled to a fraction of what it had been. The once-thriving community was forced to scale back its church programs and involvement with the Methodist Conference, but members held things together at least into the 1980s. The current owners of Rock Mill Plantation purchased the church in 2002 and have done a beautiful restoration.

The foundation of a portion of Rock Mills Church rests on large rocks like this one. Elevating the foundation in this way allowed for some circulation and ventilation inside the building in the days before air-conditioning.

The interior of the church has been as meticulously restored as the exterior. Painting has been carefully redone, accenting the trim details at the windows and wainscoting.

This photo highlights the raised apse, the prayer rail, and the communion table standing before the cross and the pulpit. The white Gothic arched windows are built into the wainscoting and contrast with the well-finished heart pine flooring.

The built-in, short pews are an unusual feature of the Rock Mills sanctuary. The rich ceiling, with slightly contrasting vertical wall planks, blends in with the white trim and natural heart pine finishes.

This is an unusual and attractive arrangement for the organ and choir. Rosette blocks at the spring point of the Gothic arched windows match the corner blocks on the door casing. Also clearly visible are the beaded vertical clapboard and wainscot details.

The Gothic-style church features lancet windows and decorative green shutters that are original to the building and have been carefully restored. The windows were constructed to open at the bottom to catch breezes in the summer months.

PHOTOGRAPHY BY TOM REED

Academy Baptist

JACKSON COUNTY ORG. 1810

According to the church website, Academy Baptist was organized in 1810 and became a member of the Sarepta Baptist Association in 1812. It is the fourth oldest Baptist church in Jackson County, after Oconee Baptist, organized in 1788, Cabin Creek (1796), and Black's Creek (1803). Among the church's leading founders was Jared Cunningham, one of the earliest white settlers in this part of Georgia. Originally from Virginia, he settled first near what is now known as Hurricane Shoals, on the North Oconee River, and later on the Middle Oconee. Academy Baptist was organized near his homestead at a location with natural springs for a water source.

In 1818 the church deacons acquired property from a man named James Appleby, who signed a deed agreeing to "relinquish, for the use of Academy Church, all rights, title and interest unto a certain lot of land containing five acres, more or less, including the Academy meeting house." This is the site of the present church, which replaced the older building in 1874. That same year, James Roberts sold additional land to the church for the price of one dollar, bringing the total size of the church's land to just under 9 acres.

The church, founded during the presidency of James Madison, is still going strong, and its congregants are working to preserve the sanctuary's historical character. A good example of their careful stewardship is the restoration of the spring-fed baptismal pool in the forest close to the church. Though no longer in use, it has been preserved as an important part of the history of Academy Baptist.

Slightly diffused light from the large nine-over-nine windows pours into the sanctuary. The double aisles point the way to the cross and lead to a perfectly proportioned chancel, with the pulpit, side chairs, and cross made of dark stained wood that stands out against the white sanctuary walls and ceiling.

The narrow tongue-and-groove walls of the apse, along with the superb window trimmings, are reminders of the skills of the local craftsmen who built this sanctuary. The elaborate chairs placed below the cross are in honor of the Trinity.

From the pulpit, the view is little changed since the church was built in 1874, during President Ulysses S. Grant's second term. The wide plank walls, windows, and hand-milled ceiling are all original. The church was built for a large congregation. The seats, backs, and ends of the center pews all came from a single plank of Georgia yellow pine.

All Baptist churches required a substantial water source for the ritual of baptism by immersion, symbolizing death, burial, and resurrection. The old Academy baptismal pool is large and well constructed. The substantial amount of water required to fill it would have come from the small creek in the background.

There are 204 recorded interments in the cemetery, and many of Jackson County's earliest white settlers rest here. This is the grave of Christopher Sailors, a Revolutionary War veteran who was born in North Carolina in 1760 and died in 1850 at the age of ninety.

PHOTOGRAPHY BY JOHN KIRKLAND

Ways Grove Baptist

JEFFERSON COUNTY ORG. 1865

We believe this is the original sanctuary of Ways Grove Baptist, one of the oldest African American churches in Georgia. The original congregants were slaves who first attended a predominantly white church, Ways Baptist, located nearby in a community then known as Stellaville.

In February 1865, two months before the fall of Richmond and the surrender at Appomattox, several of these slaves petitioned the elders of Ways Baptist to hold their own meetings. According to Doris Gunn Smith's *Ways Baptist Church, Stellaville, Georgia, Jefferson County*, the request was granted, and services were held first inside the church and later on the church grounds, with the understanding that the grounds were to be used for "religious purposes only."

In May 1867, sixteen of the newly freed slaves applied for letters granting them permission to join another Baptist church. "On Friday, June 16, 1867, this church [Ways Grove Baptist] was organized with four white friends, Rev. Kilpatrick, W.W. Rogers, W.M. Davis and James Oliphant," Smith explains. "The black members were Milo Jordan, Alfred Young, Charlie Redman, Lit Walker, Harry Benefield, George Beasley, Annie Beasley and Mariah Hannah. Rev. Alfred Young was called to pastor this little number." Smith writes that Reverend Young served Ways Grove Baptist for nearly twenty years and grew its rolls to 175 members. On March 13, 1884, the Louisville (Georgia) *News and Farmer* reported Young's death, noting that "he is said to be the only licensed colored minister that has died in this county since the war."

We believe the church pictured here was the original sanctuary of the Ways Grove church and, at various times, also served as a school and a community center. A new church was built nearby in 1888 and was encased in brick in 1952. According to Find a Grave, there are 490 documented interments in the cemetery, making it one of the larger African American graveyards in rural Georgia. Forty-six internments are of people who were born enslaved. However, a church member told us that there are also over two hundred unmarked graves, a common occurrence in older rural cemeteries, where many of the congregants were simply too poor to afford headstones. Many of these people would have been born into slavery as well.

Among those who were buried at the cemetery was Deacon Sebron (Seaborn) Brinson, who was born in 1811 and died in 1915 at the age of 104. He would have spent the first fifty-plus years of his life as a slave and was likely the property of John Brinson, the father of Stella Brinson, after whom the Stellaville community is named. In the 1880 census, Deacon Brinson listed the birthplace of his father as Africa.

The white church, Ways Baptist, goes back to 1817 and is still active, as is Ways Grove. The two churches are located less than half a mile apart in the town of Wrens.

The original Ways Grove sanctuary is a remarkably well-preserved example of a Black church of the late nineteenth century. All of the floors, walls, ceilings, window frames, doors, and pews are of pine. It is unusual to find a woodstove of this era still in place and intact.

This photo, taken from the aisle and looking at the north wall, shows that vines have crept through the windows and invaded the sanctuary. Yet these windows must be watertight since there is little or no evidence of rainwater damage, even though the north wall bears the brunt of bad weather during Georgia winters.

In this view from the south-side pews, looking toward the two six-over-six sashed windows, there is no evidence of water damage. The pews are all fairly close to the only source of heat, the woodstove in the center of the sanctuary.

Normally a rectangular brick floor would sit underneath a stove to prevent the wooden floor from catching fire. The absence of such a safeguard makes it surprising that the building never went up in flames.

Deacon Sebron (Seaborn) Brinson died May 17, 1915. Although one source gives his birthdate as 1811, the 1880 census of District 81, Jefferson County, lists "Seaborn Brinson, age 50, father born in Africa." It is rare to find the documented grave of a second-generation enslaved person in Georgia, since Congress outlawed the African slave trade in 1808.

Here lies Annie Wright Clark, born a slave in Jefferson County in 1850. Her December 9, 1920, death certificate stated that her mother's and father's birthplaces were unknown. Apoplexy was listed as the cause of death.

PHOTOGRAPHY BY RANDALL DAVIS

Fair Haven Methodist

JENKINS COUNTY ORG. 1785

Fair Haven Methodist Church was most likely organized about 1785—or possibly earlier—by members of the Jones family, whose patriarch, Francis Jones Sr., arrived in Georgia from North Carolina prior to American independence. He settled on the east side of the Ogeechee River, in what was then St. Matthew Parish, now Screven County. Francis had two sons, Francis Jr. and Philip, and it is in this pre–Revolutionary War period that the Jones family legacy and the Fair Haven church have their roots. The present church is the third one to house the congregation.

According to the National Register of Historic Places, in 1784 Francis's second son, Philip, was granted 287 acres in what is now Jenkins County as compensation for his service in the Revolutionary War. He died only a few years later, at the age of thirty, leaving behind his wife and a single heir, eighteen-month-old Henry Philip Jones.

In the decades between Philip's death and the Civil War, Henry developed the property into a profitable enterprise known as Birdsville Plantation, named after Samuel Bird, who set up the plantation's first post office in 1813. The plantation made the family very wealthy. When Henry died in 1853, his estate was valued at $350,000—in excess of $10 million in today's currency.

During the Civil War, Fair Haven Church and Birdsville Plantation lay in the path of Union general William Tecumseh Sherman's army during his March to the Sea. According to a church history, Union troops came to the church and removed a drop-leaf table, which somehow ended up at a nearby tenant farm. The resident promptly returned it to the church, unharmed except for a missing drawer. The table, absent the drawer, now occupies a prominent place on the chancel.

The interior of the sanctuary is elegant but intentionally plain, and most of the interior decorative elements are architectural. The walls are painted a shade of beige while the ceiling and pew ends are white. The eight tall windows are nestled into molded white wooden frames, while the wide board ceiling is embraced by heavy, deep crown molding, painted white as well.

The heavy, ornate pulpit rests on the raised chancel and is flanked by two ornate Victorian chairs. The drop-leaf table, which dates from the early nineteenth century, was taken by Union troops during the 1864 Savannah campaign but was ultimately returned to the church, with only a drawer missing.

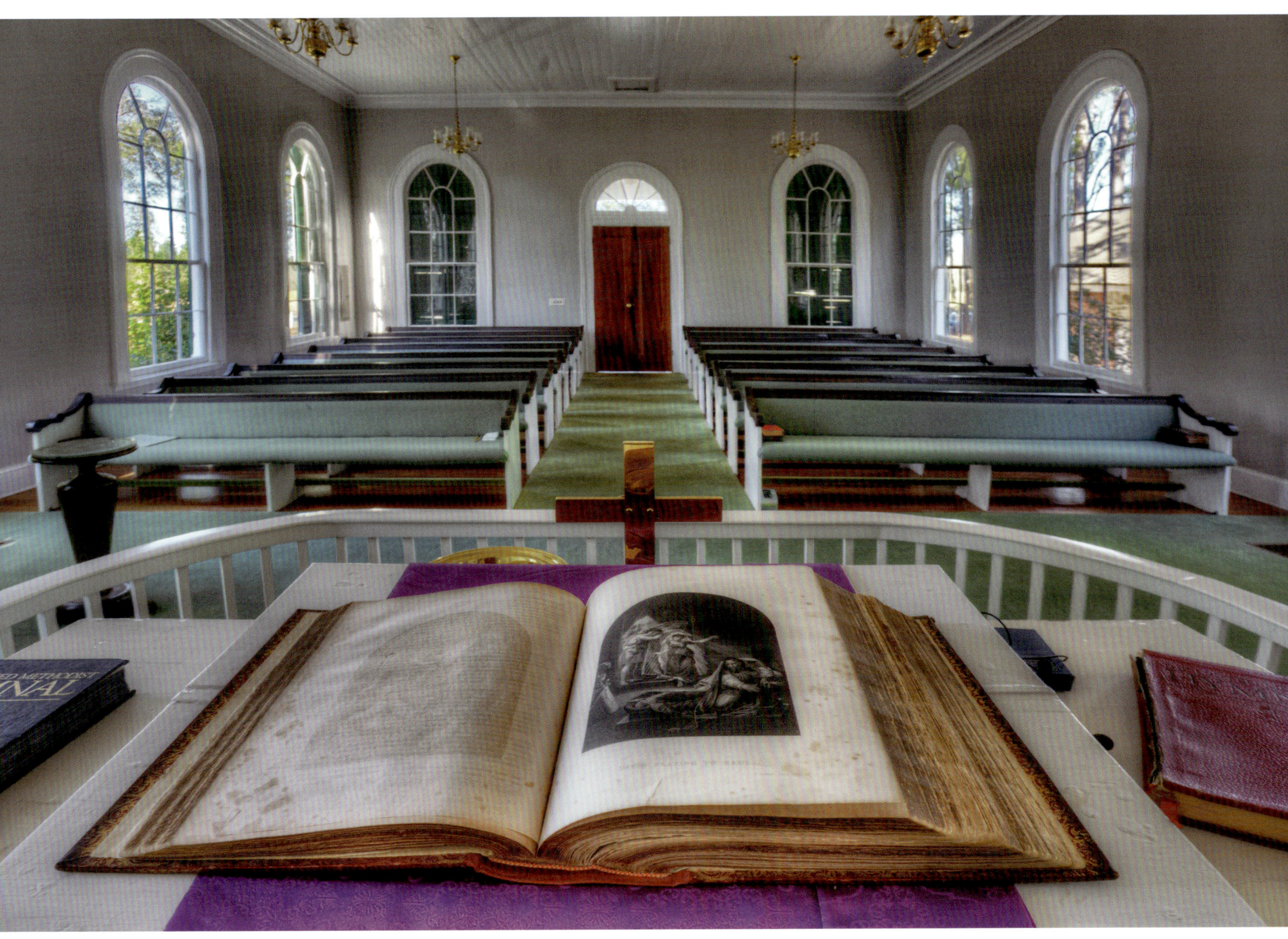

Many physical changes have been made to the sanctuary during the last century and a half, but the entryway remains as it has always been. The entry hole for the bell tower is visible in the ceiling, allowing the church bell above to be rung, just as it has for generations.

The Romanesque windows are set in elaborate wooden frames that are double hung so they can be opened to provide air circulation. Such an expensive treatment was not common in rural Georgia churches of the mid-nineteenth century.

This nineteenth-century pew, with sinuous arm rests, is perfectly fitted into the Fair Haven entry and is centered in front of a shuttered, Romanesque opening. Wide, horizontal painted boards complete the picture.

Fair Haven Methodist Church is one of the most remarkable examples of rural church architecture in Georgia. It was built with superb craftsmanship and remains in pristine condition.

PHOTOGRAPHY BY SCOTT FARRAR

Union Primitive Baptist

LAMAR COUNTY ORG. 1837

In the early nineteenth century, the Creek Nation made a series of land cessions that added to Georgia's expanding territory. Through the 1805 Treaty of Washington and the 1821 Treaty of Indian Springs, the state acquired the land first between the Oconee and Ocmulgee Rivers and then between the Ocmulgee and the Flint Rivers. Part of this territory became Monroe County, portions of which later were used to constitute Bibb, Butts, Lamar, and Pike Counties. Union Primitive Baptist was established in what is now Lamar County in 1837, on land donated by Benjamin Dumas (1783–1853) and two of his sons in the village of Goggans (Goggins), named for planter and businessman John Goggans. The first structure was a log building, soon to be replaced by a larger frame building in 1856. The present structure you see here was built in 1890.

Union's members had split off from nearby Shiloh Baptist, founded in 1826, to join a new denomination known as Primitive Baptists. The Primitive Baptists began in the 1830s when some members of the Baptist faith felt the church had become too progressive by embracing new concepts such as missions, Sunday schools, and the use of musical instruments in worship. Union is one of the earliest Primitive Baptist churches in Georgia, and its furnishings are compatible with the faith—no frills, and no musical instruments or other distractions from the original worship traditions they wished to uphold.

The cemetery is well maintained and holds the remains of some of Georgia's earliest white settlers. There are 220 documented interments, and twenty-eight of them bear the surname Dumas. In cemeteries this old, there are undoubtedly many more graves that are unmarked.

The pews, both ornate and comfortable, were made from local materials and were the products of an unusually high level of craftsmanship for the time. Wood like this Georgia heart pine is virtually unavailable today.

The Union sanctuary contains no piano or organ. In keeping with Primitive Baptist custom, all singing was done a cappella. Eventually Primitive Baptists made widespread use of the shape-note method of singing, and particularly the Sacred Harp style, which used shaped musical notes in hymnbooks to guide those singing without accompaniment.

This gas heater replaced the old wood-burning stove that was in the front of the sanctuary and provided the only heat.

Union's simple furnishings reflect the theology of the Primitive Baptist denomination.

Here lies Benjamin Franklin Dumas, one of the founders of the church, who was born August 24, 1783, in North Carolina and died here on March 1, 1853. He and Martha Ussery, whom he married in 1803, had twelve children. His marker describes Dumas as "donator of five acres for this cemetery and Union Church."

There are 221 recorded interments in the cemetery. Of these, sixty-nine are from the nineteenth century, and twenty-eight are from the Dumas family. The oldest is that of Martha Ussery Dumas, who was born in 1778 in North Carolina and died in 1838 at the age of sixty.

PHOTOGRAPHY BY WAYNE MOORE

Walthourville Presbyterian

LONG COUNTY ORG. 1855

Walthourville Presbyterian had its roots in Midway Congregational Church, organized in 1752 by descendants of Puritans migrating into southeastern Georgia from Dorchester, South Carolina. They were among the settlers receiving grants from the Georgia colonial government totaling nearly 32,000 acres, in exchange for creating a southern buffer against the Creeks and the Spanish for the emerging port of Savannah. Another factor encouraging their migration was that in 1751 the Georgia colony lifted its prohibition against slavery, making it profitable for rice to be grown in the Georgia Low Country. Within twenty years some sixty planters, who owned roughly half the colony's rapidly expanding slave population, dominated the Georgia rice economy.

Because malaria was prevalent in the low swampy areas around the village of Midway, where many plantations were located, plantation owners built summer homes in what they termed the pinelands to avoid the increased threat of malaria each summer. Walthourville was one of three "retreat churches" associated with Midway Congregational, the mother church organized in 1752. The other two were Flemington Presbyterian, organized in 1815, and Dorchester Presbyterian, organized in 1854—both located in Liberty County.

Congregants of the Walthourville church initially met in an 1820 meeting house that served both Baptists and Presbyterians. In 1845, a new building was erected. The 1845 sanctuary burned in 1877 and was replaced by a new church on land purchased from the Walthour estate. That structure was destroyed by a storm in 1881 and was replaced in 1884 by the building pictured here.

In 1855, thirty-three members of Midway were dismissed to form a separate and independent church. They voted overwhelmingly to join the Presbyterian Church, rather than to retain the Congregational form of government. By 1861, Walthourville Presbyterian had the second-largest congregation in the presbytery and ranked first in benevolent giving. *Liberty County, Georgia: A Pictorial History* notes that in the late 1850s, "a small building was erected for the colored people where they had services and the women in the church conducted Sunday School for them."

In 1872, land was donated by Captain William Bacon to be set apart for use as a public cemetery. There are presently 361 documented interments in the cemetery, which include some of the earliest white settlers in the Georgia Low Country. Captain Bacon died in 1905 and is buried in the cemetery.

A low, continuous wooden wainscot is used throughout the sanctuary. Above it are replicas of a gas-powered sconce and a chandelier, as well as an octagonal, nineteenth-century regulator schoolhouse clock.

This view from the pulpit shows, on the left, two Gothic lancet windows and a single replica gas lantern, just like the originals used in the sanctuary. In the background are steps leading to the original, wainscoted gallery, which is supported by two large columns. The large chandelier in the center is a replica of the gas original.

The upholstered love seat at the center of the apse is an unusual element but provides a nice focal point. The apse windows are shorter than the main lancet windows but still allow abundant light to flood the alcove.

This photo, taken from the gallery above the main floor, shows a large number of the original pews, as well as the choir area and organ. The apse rests beneath and behind proscenium-like green drapes while receiving much light through its three windows.

Old books and pamphlets line the shelves of this cabinet at Walthourville.

This impressive headstone marks the grave of Edward Payson Miller (1840–1910). He enlisted early in the Civil War, and following Appomattox, he continued to serve Georgia in a volunteer military capacity, retiring as a colonel. He is listed in the 1910 census as a turpentine manufacturer.

PHOTOGRAPHY BY BRYAN STOVALL

St. Andrew's Episcopal

MCINTOSH COUNTY ORG. 1841

St. Andrew's was first organized as St. Peter's in 1841, but the name was changed the following year. The original sanctuary, completed in 1844, was a wooden structure located about two hundred feet north of the present one, in the coastal town of Darien. The present church, of classic fourteenth-century English architectural style, was completed in 1879. The story of St. Andrew's is deeply rooted in Georgia coastal history, as well as the history of the Butler family. Much of that history is recorded in *Major Butler's Legacy: Five Generations of a Slaveholding Family* by Malcolm Bell Jr.

Located on the banks of the Altamaha River, Darien was founded by Scottish Highlanders in 1736, two years after the founding of Savannah. It prospered as a seaport during the eighteenth and early nineteenth centuries but, in the 1830s, railroads began to radically change the commercial transportation system of Georgia's agricultural economy. The rail line routes that were selected bypassed Darien, taking cotton directly to Savannah for export. The Bank of Darien failed in 1841, and the town's fortunes began to sink with it. In 1863, during the Civil War, Union troops burned Darien to the ground, including St. Andrew's Church.

The church was rebuilt in 1879 through the efforts of an English clergyman, the Reverend James W. Leigh, who married Frances Kemble Butler in Philadelphia in 1871. Frances was the great-granddaughter of Pierce Butler, an Irish nobleman and a major in the British Army, who married the daughter of a wealthy South Carolina planter in 1771. He resigned his commission and sided with the American colonists during the Revolutionary War. After the war, he had a career as a prominent statesman and a planter, including serving three terms in the U.S. Senate. He established large plantations on St. Simons Island and Butler Island, just across the river from Darien, where he became one of the wealthiest men in America and one of the largest slaveholders.

Upon Major Butler's death in 1822, Frances's father, Pierce Mease Butler, inherited a significant portion of his grandfather's wealth but quickly squandered it. By 1859 he was so deeply in debt that he notoriously sold off a large number of enslaved people—436 men, women, and children—from the plantations. Held in Savannah in early March 1859, it was one of the largest slave auctions in U.S. history and came to be known as "the Weeping Time."

After her father's death in 1867, Frances and her husband moved from their home in Philadelphia to run the plantation she had inherited. In 1874, Reverend Leigh engaged an architect—a fellow Englishman—to design a new Episcopal church to be located across the river in Darien. The plans were based on a fourteenth-century Gothic stone church located near Manchester, England. The church was built on the former site of the Bank of Darien, with local timber coming down the Altamaha River to the sawmills in Darien.

The interior of St. Andrew's, modeled on a fourteenth-century Gothic English church, features a medieval-style trussed rafter roof system with arch-braced support.

Since Darien was the epicenter of the heart pine industry in the nineteenth century, it is not surprising the entire sanctuary is constructed from that type of wood, finished in a golden-brown stain.

The walls, roof, window frames, leaded glass, furniture, and decorative accessories are of the highest order and reflect the wealth of the congregants.

The structural bones and design elements make this church one of the most unusual in rural Georgia.

Originally a family burial ground, the St. Andrew's cemetery is on land donated in 1867 by the son of Thomas Spalding, the owner of Sapelo Island and one of the wealthiest planters on the Georgia coast. Today, there are over 1,500 graves in the cemetery.

Cemeteries reflect the economic status of the people buried there. The mausoleum on the right holds the remains of William Churchill (1811–88), born in England. Census records show he was a merchant as well as a planter. The granite obelisk in the center marks the grave of Adam Strain (1840–97), who enlisted in the Confederacy as a young man and made his money after the war as a merchant. The marble Victorian angel on the left marks the plot of the Schmidt family. Carl August Schmidt (1837–1914) was born in Germany, served in the war, and made his money as a "timber merchant." He was also president of the Bank of Darien.

PHOTOGRAPHY BY WAYNE MOORE

Wayfair Primitive Baptist

MCINTOSH COUNTY ORG. 1873

Wayfair Primitive Baptist is located only a few miles from St. Andrew's, but it provides a sharp contrast in style and architecture and represents a very different aspect of Georgia history. Like Brantley County's Bethlehem Church, also featured in this book, Wayfair is located in the Wiregrass Region, deep in southeast Georgia—a hot, sandy environment that is poorly suited for many types of agriculture. According to John Crowley's 1998 book, *Primitive Baptists of the Wiregrass South: 1815 to the Present*, this part of the Wiregrass Region was initially populated by poor Scots-Irish settlers who made a living any way they could. On the other hand, St. Andrew's was situated on the Georgia marsh, where eighteenth- and nineteenth-century fortunes were made in rice and cotton.

The Primitive Baptist denomination began in the 1830s when its members broke away from the Baptist Church, believing it to be too progressive. They were opposed to mission boards, Sunday schools, and other religious elements not explicitly outlined in Scripture. They adopted the word *primitive* to imply "original," claiming they were modeling themselves after the earliest adherents of Christianity.

Within the Primitive Baptist movement was a faction known as "Crawfordites," led by a charismatic elder named Reuben Crawford. All Crawfordite meetinghouses were built of the same materials, had the same floor plan, and were unpainted. Wayfair Primitive Baptist was one such church. As time passed, many Primitive Baptist congregations began to improve their buildings, but the Crawfordites saw comfort as a distraction from worship. That view persists today, and the few remaining Crawfordite meetinghouses appear much as they did in the nineteenth century.

All Crawfordite meetinghouses were constructed in a consistent way, with tin roofs, exposed rafters, and three entrances. The main entrance opened onto a center aisle that went from the double door to the stand (pulpit). The single entry doors were separated by gender: women on the right from the stand, and men on the left. This view shows the women's entrance.

On the men's side, to the left of the stand, is a simple plank suspended from the rafters with nails protruding to serve as a hat rack. In the floor are small, circular holes that served the members who chewed tobacco.

In Crawfordite churches the stand, or pulpit, is always in the center back and is for elders only. A bench is there, too, since sometimes multiple elders speak. Another bench, or sometimes a chair, is always placed in front of the stand for the recorder. The raised cover on the floor in front of the stand is for the disposal of water during the foot-washing ritual, an important part of Primitive Baptist worship.

These simple bench pews are similar to those used in all Crawfordite meetinghouses.

This is the double-door main entrance to the stand where elders preach. Elders do not prepare sermons or use outlines or notes. Instead, they speak extemporaneously. There are no musical instruments of any kind, since Primitive Baptists do their singing a cappella.

PHOTOGRAPHY BY GAIL DES JARDIN SEGARS

Odessadale Methodist

MERIWETHER COUNTY ORG. 1897

The little farming community of Odessadale, in the rural backcountry between LaGrange and Greenville in Meriwether County, has been around for almost two hundred years, even though the town was not incorporated until 1905. According to Kenneth Krakow's *Georgia Place-Names*, the community was first known as Xerxes, named after the plantation of Henry Richard Harris (1781–1858). His son, Colonel Henry Richard Harris (1828–1909), was a member of the original Odessadale congregation, and his son's wife, Kate Virginia Moses Harris, was its first Sunday school superintendent.

Odessadale Methodist was organized in the late 1800s in a schoolhouse by members of the Methodist church in Mountville, a short distance away, but still a significant ride in a horse and buggy. Odessa Thompson, a prominent member of the Odessa Baptist Church and the woman for whom the town is named, donated an acre and a half for the church and a school.

Members of the congregation, led by Cornelius Harman, designed and built the church structure. Their skill is reflected in the unusual entryway, offset bell tower, and interior craftsmanship. Many members of the Harman family are buried in the church cemetery. Cornelius's great-grandson, Gaines Harman, is an active member of the congregation and was our primary source of information about the church.

In 2016, the sanctuary was endangered when the original foundation piers began to disintegrate. With funds donated by Gaines Harman and other parishioners, the piers were repaired and the failing walls stabilized using steel cabling to pull them upright and straight.

Cornelius Harman and several other members made the prayer rail, the balustrade with classic turned balusters and kneeling pad, and the pews. At one time the interior walls were covered with wallpaper, but church members in the 1940s decided to remove it and refinish the original wood.

The handmade pews are original, and the double-aisle floor plan means the short pews are built flush to the wainscoting. The horizontal plank walls above the wainscoting are in contrast with the white ceiling. Stained-glass windows replaced clear ones in the 1960s. The window on the left is dedicated to the parents of Gaines Harman.

A children's corner, which sits on the left side of the church, next to the chancel, allows children to gather in their own chairs and speak with an adult, pastor, or special guest. These bentwood oak chairs were originally used in the schoolhouse.

This stained-glass window is dedicated to the memory of Johnnie Glanton, a young girl who died in 1896 at the age of six.

Of the 113 interments in the graveyard, twenty-five carry the surname Harman. Among them is Merriman Harman (1841–1929). According to *Roster of the Confederate Soldiers of Georgia*, Harman enlisted as a private in March 1862, was captured at Baker's Creek, Mississippi, in May 1863, and was paroled at Fort Delaware in July 1863. At the end of the war, the *Roster* adds, "pension records show he was on detail duty with wagon train at Newberry, S.C."

PHOTOGRAPHY BY CATE SHORT

Swords Methodist

MORGAN COUNTY ORG. 1912

Swords, a small, rural community in Morgan County, has its roots in the entrepreneurial spirit of John Buchanon "Buck" Swords (1859–1940). The community developed near Blue Springs, named for the natural water sources that were essential to the early success of Buck's primary business, Swords Distillery.

Formally incorporated by the Georgia legislature on August 16, 1909, Swords developed a commercial center that included a general supply store, gristmill, cotton gin, and blacksmith shop. However, by the 1920s, Prohibition brought about the demise of the distillery and, ultimately, the town.

In 1912, several years before the Eighteenth Amendment would bring such dramatic change to their village, residents launched an ambitious effort to build a Methodist church. "A committee is now at work getting up subscriptions [financial pledges], and work will soon be begun," reported the *Madisonian* newspaper, based in nearby Madison, on September 6, 1912. "The people want a $2,000 church, and we feel sure with so many willing ones to help, the amount will soon be on hand."

The new church was dedicated less than ten months later. "Last Sunday, June 29, will be remembered pleasantly by all who attended the dedication of the beautiful new Methodist church at Swords, Ga.," wrote the *Madisonian* on July 4, 1913. "Dr. [James Edward] Dickey, [the president of Emory College], preached one of the most magnificent sermons ever heard. It may more perfectly be termed a revelation. The hospitality of Mr. J. B. Swords and many of the good people of that community was a marked feature . . . of the occasion."

Although the Swords community is no longer incorporated, the church remains intact, with an active congregation. Rural Georgia has many of these once-vibrant towns and villages that have slowly disappeared—leaving only the churches, the graveyards, and a few old buildings to remind us of days gone by.

The church was built in 1913 to serve a community that had prospered due to the success of Swords Distillery, then a rival of Jack Daniels. Prohibition spelled the end of the distillery and most of the town, but the church has survived virtually intact.

This close-up of the chancel and pulpit area shows the wainscot, the turned balusters of the prayer rail, and other elements that look much as they did when the church was built over one hundred years ago.

The theater seats located on either side of the sanctuary feature more ornate woodwork and cast-iron side pieces than those in the center section. The seats are original to the church, and we are not sure why two styles were used.

Clever "hat racks" placed beneath the seats kept men's hats safe and out of the way during services. We have not seen this feature in any other rural Georgia church.

The ceiling with its narrow heart pine ceiling boards, the wainscot, and the elaborately framed stained-glass windows are proof of the congregation's intent to build the best sanctuary they could afford.

Two Gothic windows near the choir area and a matching pair on the opposite wall complement the main arched window at the front of the church. The stained glass casts a green glow throughout the sanctuary.

John Buchanon "Buck" Swords was born in Carroll County, Georgia, in 1859. His father was killed in 1864 during the Confederate defense of Atlanta. From this difficult beginning, Buck became one of the most successful early twentieth-century entrepreneurs in this part of Georgia. He owned the J. B. Swords Supply Company and the Swords Distillery and was president of the J. B. Swords Bank. This 1899 photo shows him with his wife, Su, and daughter, Jessie.

PHOTOGRAPHY BY STEVE ROBINSON

Hopewell Missionary Baptist

QUITMAN COUNTY ORG. 1876

According to *Cemeteries and Churches of Quitman County, Georgia* by Jacquelyn M. Shepard, Hopewell Missionary Baptist was organized in 1876, and its members met in a brush arbor for about the first ten years. Its first pastor was Reverend Dixon, and its first deacon was Croff Crumbley. The church pictured here was completed in 1886.

The structure is in remarkable condition, given the congregation is inactive and has been for years. The tin roof is relatively new, and the sanctuary is in good condition as a result. As with so many other rural churches across Georgia, the members may have been poor, but they were skilled at working with the materials they had—mostly trees and rocks.

Hopewell is in a remote location, and it is striking that there are no houses anywhere near the church. However, given that the early congregants attended by foot and by horse, there must have been a vibrant community around the church in days gone by. Like other African American churches founded in the years following the Civil War, it would have played an important role in the lives of newly freed slaves and their children.

Hopewell is a remarkable example of an early African American church, organized shortly after the Civil War, that served its community well for many years. As the United States began to industrialize at the turn of the century, opportunities for a better life and better jobs emerged in the larger cities, especially in the North, resulting in declining rural populations. Georgia now has 159 counties, and Quitman County ranks 158th in terms of population and 152nd in per-capita income.

This close-up view of the front of the church shows the chancel, pulpit area, and apse. The unusual theater-like drapes above the apse create a proscenium.

Except for some water damage in the ceiling, the sanctuary appears to be in remarkable condition, even though it has been abandoned for years.

This view from the pulpit has not changed much since the church's inception. Many sermons have been delivered from this spot.

In the days before air-conditioning was widely available, handheld fans were a staple in churches throughout the South. This one at Hopewell pays tribute to Dr. Martin Luther King Jr.

All of Hopewell's footings are constructed of hand-dug fieldstones. These unmortared fieldstones have kept the church plumb and level, even after 135 years.

The little graveyard beside the church contains one hundred documented interments, according to Find a Grave. However, there are undoubtedly many unmarked graves here as well. Death certificates for Quitman County show several people buried at Hopewell between 1919 and 1929 with no findable markers.

PHOTOGRAPHY BY STEVE ROBINSON

Phillippi Primitive Baptist

SCHLEY COUNTY ORG. 1835

On a lonely and remote dirt road in rural Schley County stands Phillippi Primitive Baptist Church, organized in 1835. Time and neglect have taken their toll, but the building still stands and reminds us of another time when Phillippi was the largest church in the Upatoi Primitive Baptist Association, with 125 members and 5 ordained elders. The old minutes still exist and tell us much about the rural community that thrived here in Schley County. The last service held at the church was in November 1978.

Much of our information about Phillippi comes from *History of Schley County, Georgia* by Mrs. H. J. Williams. It provides rich details from church records. For example, the minutes of September 30, 1837, outline the theological justification for breaking away from the Baptist Church and joining the new Primitive Baptist denomination: "Wheras, there are certain characters who call themselves Missionaries, arisen in the Baptist denomination, and are forming Institutions, which we believe to be contrary to the word of God, viz. Missionary, Bible, Tract and Temperance Societies, Theological Seminaries, and Baptist Colleges. Resolved therefore that we declare a non-fellowship with said institutions and with all engaged in them. We further resolve that we do not invite or suffer a Baptist preacher, known to be friendly to, or engaged in said institutions, to preach in our meeting house."

Additional minutes from 1837 disclose that a male member was excommunicated for getting drunk, while another was brought up for trial before the church for visiting a Masonic lodge. Still others were excommunicated for taking a homestead to avoid payment of honest debts. At the same time, the records stress the doors of the church were opened at each monthly meeting for the reception of members, both white and Black. The minutes dated March 1, 1835, tell us, "Randall Stewart and Lotty, a black sister, were received into the full fellowship of the church, by letter."

The durability of these old handmade structures is remarkable—still standing after being abandoned for decades. Phillippi is one of the churches that fall in the category we refer to as "Almost Gone but Not Forgotten." It has a proud history that reminds us of the important role rural churches like this played in Georgia's early nineteenth-century history.

Though the meetinghouse appears to be in dramatic disrepair when viewed from outside, this view of the chancel and pulpit area reveals a sanctuary interior in relatively good condition. Although the windows, frames, and doors are gone, the heart pine ceiling, walls, and floorboards are mostly sound.

Usually abandoned churches have been devastated by weather damage, vandalism, or materials' scavengers. But other than the dismantling and removal of the pulpit and some chancel boards, Phillippi's interior remains intact. We guess that the church's isolation has helped keep damage to a minimum.

The tin roof is still watertight, and the heart pine siding, framing, floors, and joists remain sound, despite rain blowing in through the open windows and doors and the decades-long lack of maintenance.

There are 101 documented interments in the graveyard, 30 percent of them from before 1900. As we frequently mention, a cemetery this old will also contain many unmarked graves.

Here lies Sara Samantha Lightner (1852–86). According to Find a Grave, she died of dysentery and "suffered a great deal." She left four living children, the youngest of whom, Katie, was eight months old. She was buried beside her daughter, Mary Ollie, who had died in 1881 at the age of one and a half.

PHOTOGRAPHY BY JOHN KIRKLAND

Bethel Brick Methodist

SCREVEN COUNTY ORG. 1827

Bethel Brick Methodist is both the oldest Methodist church and the oldest church building in Screven County. Services have been held continuously in the building since 1827. The original structure, now almost two hundred years old, is still in good condition and continues to serve an active congregation.

The church owes its origins to the Maner and Wade families, who were among the wealthiest planters in post–Revolutionary War Georgia. Sam Maner was a veteran of that war who moved across the Savannah River from South Carolina in 1812. He bought 2,523 acres from George and Mary Williamson in Screven County and built a new home and plantation, naming it Lebanon Forest.

Maner died around 1816 and left the plantation to his daughter Sarah and her husband, the Reverend John Crawford. After Crawford died just a few years later, Sarah married another Methodist preacher, the Reverend Peyton Lisby Wade. Since neither marriage produced any children, the property passed to Wade upon Sarah's death in 1838. Wade then married his late wife's niece, Elizabeth Robert, twenty-two years his junior. Together they had eleven children and expanded their land holdings to over 10,000 acres. At one time Reverend Wade enslaved as many as five hundred people.

In 1827, prior to Sarah's death, Wade conveyed to seven trustees a deed for 2¾ acres of land to build a Methodist Episcopal church to be known as "Brick Church." Enslaved people from Lebanon Forest Plantation built the structure. Before the Civil War, the church counted more Black members than white. The 1859 annual conference minutes showed 150 white members and 418 Black members. Such a ratio was not unusual in the heart of Georgia's plantation country. The white members held Sunday morning worship services, and the Black members worshipped on Sunday afternoons.

Although Bethel Brick's sanctuary has seen many modifications in the past two hundred years, the simplicity of its original design has been maintained.

This type of semicircular altar rail and balustrade on a two-level chancel and pulpit area is typical for many rural churches but would have been uncommon in the 1820s.

The wide, double-door entryway is probably just as it was when the church was constructed. The elaborate window frames and ornate stained glass, on the other hand, are part of later alterations.

This stained-glass window, though colorful and attractive, is not of the same quality as the Tiffany, La Farge, or Lamb windows it is imitating.

Fourteen members of the Wade family are interred at Bethel Brick. Four of Reverend Wade's sons served in the Civil War. Robert and Ulysses survived, but Edward was wounded at the Battle of Sailor's Creek and died in a Union prison camp. Peyton Wade enlisted early in the conflict at the age of twenty and died of an unknown disease on his twenty-first birthday.

We are not sure when this tribute to Reverend Wade was erected. That a man of the cloth could enslave hundreds of people is difficult to understand today, but Wade was not unusual in this respect. Many church leaders and members of the clergy owned large numbers of slaves.

PHOTOGRAPHY BY BRYAN STOVALL AND RANDALL DAVIS

Walker Grove Baptist

SCREVEN COUNTY ORG. 1900 (EST.)

Little is known about the history of Walker Grove Church and School, although we estimate they were organized around 1900. Both were part of the Pilgrim Missionary Baptist Association, based in Guyton. The association began in 1868, shortly after emancipation, to help member congregations with problems and issues of the day. A major concern had to do with education, since public schooling was then unavailable to African American students. In response, churches established one- or two-room schools to serve students in the elementary grades. Walker Grove, in the village of Newington, was one such school.

When the Historic Rural Churches of Georgia project first documented Walker Grove in 2018, both the church and the school were abandoned and falling into serious disrepair. It was too late to intervene on behalf of the school, but fortunately a local resident, Zandra Overstreet, and colleagues at the Newington Heritage Society decided to try and save the church. Despite limited funds, they worked diligently through the COVID-19 pandemic to breathe life back into this historic building. In 2022, the church opened its doors for the first time in decades. Photos on these pages show the building before and after the renovation.

The renovation effort had the goal of saving as much of the original church as possible, and it succeeded admirably. Everything in this photo is original, and the sanctuary looks much as it would have in the early 1900s.

A choir loft, with room for eight, is enclosed by a low wall and connected to the chancel. The pulpit appears to be original, as does the raised chancel.

Water damage to the roof had caused the cellulose ceiling panels to become saturated and fall away from the ceiling in two areas, revealing the beaded tongue-and-groove paneling. The original pews are simple in construction but substantial. The vaulted suspended-truss ceiling has unusually long shoulders, giving it a more pronounced cathedral-like impression.

Black history has long been emphasized in schools serving African American students. For example, in 1933 the Tennessee State Association of Teachers in Colored Schools asserted in its journal *Broadcaster*, "Since pride of race is one of the most powerful incentives to noble effort, the good deeds of individual Negroes and the contributions to civilization of the race as a whole should be taught in every school for Negroes." These photos of prominent Black figures, posted on the wall at Walker Grove Church, reflect that resolve to instill its young members with pride.

Here is one of the photos taken before the renovation. The double-tower configuration is a common architectural feature of African American churches. These towers take many forms, but a single entry centered between the towers is often seen in many old churches.

Walker Grove School was a two-room schoolhouse with a wood heater in each room. Abandoned long ago, it is in such poor condition that it cannot be renovated.

PHOTOGRAPHY BY STEVE ROBINSON

Providence Methodist

STEWART COUNTY ORG. 1832

Providence Methodist was founded in 1832 on 2 acres of land donated by the Reverend David Lowe. The first structure, a log building, was replaced in 1859 by the present structure, which sits on 2 acres of land across the road. It is one of the oldest churches in the county and has been preserved virtually intact. It has some distinctive construction features, including a hipped roof, which was unusual for the time.

The church is located in what is now Providence Canyon State Park, named after the church. The so-called canyons, sixteen in all, are billed as a tourist attraction and often referred to as Georgia's Little Grand Canyon. But unlike geological formations in the western United States that developed over millions of years, these gorges in Stewart County were created in the 1800s by poor farming practices. Massive erosion in the soft, unstable subsurface became the canyons of today in a relatively short period of time. In Georgia, an abundance of cheap land often led to many years of agrarian abuse.

According to local historians, Providence Methodist sits on a road that was formerly a trail used by Indigenous people. The last land cession by the Creeks took place in 1825 at the conclusion of the Second Treaty of Indian Springs. Legal settlement began with the state's fifth land lottery, held in 1827. However, clashes between the white settlers and the Creeks were still occurring at the time of Providence Methodist's organization.

In 1836, some of the dissident Creeks began ambushing homes and communities in a desperate struggle to retain their hunting grounds. The settlers called on Governor William Schley for protection. On June 9 of that year, Creek warriors fought members of the Georgia militia at the Battle of Shepherd's Plantation in Stewart County not far from the church. It was one of the bloodiest engagements of the Creek War of 1836.

Church minutes from 1861 reveal that thirty-seven enslaved people were members of Providence Methodist at that time. The cemetery contains the marked graves of many original settlers, as well as unmarked graves that were once identified with wooden markers or fieldstones that have disappeared over time.

Both the floorboards and the hand-hewn pews are of longleaf pine, the dominant tree in this area of Georgia. The pews are joined using the ancient mortise-and-tenon technique—no nails or screws. Wood-burning stoves like the one in this photo served as the primary heat source in every one of these early churches.

The chancel has likely been modified and upgraded along with the molded window frames, but the original doors remain in use. The vertical and horizontal wall and ceiling boards look much as they did when they were installed in 1859.

We seldom find a church, active or abandoned, that still has an old woodstove in the sanctuary. This one is particularly intriguing, but so far we have been unable to learn anything about when or where it was manufactured.

Old churches were usually lit by ceiling-mounted oil lanterns and wall sconces that disappeared when electric lighting became available in these remote villages. The Providence sanctuary is one of the very few where old-style lamps remain the only lighting source.

The fenced burial plot above is the final resting place of the Duskin family. The grave in the foreground is that of Sergeant Michael Duskin (1840–1911), who served with the Second Georgia Infantry. The grave in the background is that of his wife, Jane Keith Duskin (1841–1908). The couple were married in 1865 when Michael returned from the war. They had four children, only one of whom lived beyond the age of thirteen.

Buried here is George Keith (December 8, 1825–January 18, 1862), who married Mary Humber in Alabama in 1847. The Stewart County 1860 census lists George W. Keith, age thirty-three; his wife, Mary, age thirty; and three children, ages seven, three, and six months. He owned fifteen slaves in 1860. Mary apparently died shortly after this census was taken, and George married Mariah Jane Perkins on October 27, 1860.

PHOTOGRAPHY BY STEVE ROBINSON

Friendship Baptist

SUMTER COUNTY ORG. 1839

Friendship Baptist was established in 1839. The present building, located in northwestern Sumter County, was built in 1857 and is the oldest standing church in the county. It was also the church of President Jimmy Carter's great-great-grandfather, Wyley Carter, who joined in 1852, shortly after moving with his family from Warren County to Sumter County. Wyley was a wealthy planter, and according to Jeff Carter's *Ancestors of Jimmy and Rosalynn Carter* and 1849 tax records, Wyley "owned twenty-nine slaves and more than 5,642 acres of land" in several counties.

Much of our knowledge about Friendship's history comes from the church minutes of 1839 to 1872, which were preserved—with their original punctuation and spelling—through the efforts of Mrs. Scott Hart of Schley County and Jack F. Cox of Americus. These minutes provide rich details about the church's earliest years and provide a glimpse into the lives of those who worshipped within its walls. A few excerpts from these minutes follow.

April 1840—The first mention of new white and Black members—"The church met and after pray meting the conference was opend for the reception of members when came forward sister Rebecca Boyet and sister Eliza a woman of color and brother James & Titus men of culler and was recd [received] all being members from Liberty church whom we know to be in good standing bowth in faith and practice."

January 16, 1841—The first mention of unacceptable behavior—"Brother Sraford an alagation against Brother Kneel Gillas of intoxication and agread to lay it over until the conference in April. Brother Staford prepared an Alagation against Jesse Parker for drawing a knife and quaraling agreed to lay it over to the next conference."

May 27, 1848—Prevarication and intoxication—"Prefered to charges against John Teal one for intoxication and the other for prevarication. . . . Took up the case of Mrs. Heath and after some discussion being had on the case She was expelled From all the privilages of the church For intoxication."

August 5, 1852—Wyley Carter's servant joins the church—"Received by letter Lucy a servant the property of Wiley Carter."

August 24, 1852—Wyley Carter and his wife, Sarah, join the church—"Rec'd by letter Wiley Carter and his wife Sarah Carter."

August 21, 1869—Emancipated slaves are still joining the church—"Rec'd by an experience of Grace Sally Lansley & Emma Collier collered, Frances Deconey colored, Louiza May, colored, Caroline May, colored, Rosetta May, colored Artemoers Worty all collored."

September 25, 1869—State of the church report given, showing that nearly 30 percent of the members are Black—"Whites in Fellowship 85, Blacks in Fellowship 35."

October 22, 1870—Most of the freed slaves now leave to start their own church—"Ordered the clerk to give Letters of Dismission to all collered members who is in fellowship with the church for the purpose of constituting a Church of their own coller."

This pattern of separation from the white segregated churches was repeated all over Georgia and the South after the war, but each church had to create its own solution. Sometimes that separation did not take place until well into the 1870s. The Friendship minutes give us a sense of that difficult process.

Built in 1857, Friendship is the oldest standing church in Sumter County. Upon entering the sanctuary, you realize that the view has not changed much.

The piano does not appear to be original and is probably one of many used in the sanctuary since 1857.

Spare Windsor chairs sit behind a simple, straight-legged communion table. On the raised chancel are three Victorian, high-backed horsehair chairs. The apse is a simple opening, encased by a wood frame, above which rises a plain wooden cross.

SUNDAY SCHOOL
OFFERING
LAST SUNDAY
650·00

If we removed the modern elements such as electric lights, thermostats, and carpeting, we would be looking at an authentic, mid-nineteenth-century meetinghouse.

Eleven graves in the cemetery have the surname Dodson. Here lies Martha Murray Dodson, who married William C. Dodson in 1859. Her tombstone refers to her as William's "relict," or widow. William was the son of Joel Dodson (1813–80), who owned twenty slaves in 1860, according to the census. William himself was a lieutenant in the Confederate army and died March 5, 1863. He too is buried in the cemetery.

The African American cemetery, New Bethel, is adjacent to the white cemetery, and graves with the surname Dodson are in both. One of those buried at New Bethel is Phebe Dodson (1868–1942), born in Madison County, Alabama, who married Green Dodson in Sumter County in 1886. Green was born between 1855 and 1860, according to county census records, and was likely one of twenty slaves belonging to Joel Dodson. Many Georgia cemeteries are connected with common surnames in this way.

PHOTOGRAPHY BY TONY CANTRELL

Corinth Methodist

TALBOT COUNTY ORG. 1828

Corinth Methodist was organized in the late 1820s, as this part of Georgia was expanding into lands previously held by Creek Indians. Robert H. Jordan's *There Was a Land: A History of Talbot County, Georgia* tells us that the Reverend James Stockdale, the newly appointed missionary to Talbot and Harris counties, crossed the Flint River and

> inquired of the ferryman if he knew of any Methodists in the area. The ferryman directed him to Josiah Mathews . . . and together they rode over the country looking for Methodists with a view to organizing a church.
>
> They found few, for the drawing of the lands west of the Flint River had been but two months and Indians were still about. Word was then circulated to meet in an unoccupied log dwelling located near the Champion house of today. A church was organized on the first day and named Corinth. Thus, the first church in the "New Purchase" territory came into being.

This group of Methodists used rough post oak logs to erect their first building, which measured approximately 16 by 20 feet. The second building, made of split pine logs, was larger, at 26 by 32 feet. In 1838, the Reverend B. R. Searcy designed the church's third structure, a frame building that was erected at a cost of $475.

The congregation continued to worship in Reverend Searcy's building for about three decades, until one particularly chilly day when, according to Methodist church history, the Reverend R. J. Corley came to preach at Corinth. Corley found that the building was more like a barn than a sanctuary, so cold the water froze on the pulpit. While the pastor, who had served four years as a private in the Confederate army, was able to keep himself warm during his fervent sermon, the congregation shivered throughout. The members soon moved to build a new structure a mile away, in what was then called Prattsburg, and raised $1,625 to construct it. Contractor James Cottingham took only thirty days to complete the project and, on October 24, 1869, Reverend Corley presided over a dedication ceremony for a church of seventy-five members.

Portions of the church were renovated leading up to a centennial celebration on August 2, 1928. By 1965, a rapid decline in the rural population led Corinth Methodist Church to consolidate with nearby Collinsworth Methodist Church. Alternating services are now held at both churches.

Other than the carpet and the electric lights, Corinth looks like an authentic, mid-nineteenth-century church that is virtually intact. The church is a classic four-column Greek Revival structure, with double entry doors, double aisles, and partitioned pews for the separation of men from women and children.

As in many Methodist churches, Windsor chairs are placed on the two-tiered chancel behind the pulpit to provide seating for dignitaries and to pay homage to the Trinity.

The snow-white walls contrast with the dark finish of the woodwork. The pews, floor, and raised chancel with prayer rail have a matching color finish, as do the communion table and pulpit.

Farrand organs were first manufactured in Detroit under this company name in 1897. The firm specialized in reed organs, as opposed to pipe organs.

The foundation of Corinth Church rests on stacks of native fieldstones pulled from the surrounding property. Different sizes were used to create the perfect balance, and the church has been level since 1869.

PHOTOGRAPHY BY SCOTT FARRAR

Zion Episcopal

TALBOT COUNTY ORG. 1847

Located in the upper Chattahoochee Valley, not far from the Alabama border, Zion Episcopal Church was organized in 1847 as a missionary church under the direction of the Reverend Richard Johnson. The current structure was built around 1848 using money from wealthy South Carolina planters. It is, in the words of those nominating it to the National Register of Historic Places, "a superb example of a small, wooden country church in the English Gothic style of the Tudor period and as interpreted in the mid 19th century."

Zion Episcopal is located in Talbotton, founded in 1828 as the seat of Talbot County. In the mid-nineteenth century it was a center of commerce and education—home to both Talbotton Female Academy (later LeVert College) and Collinsworth Institute. The most famous graduates of Collinsworth were Nathan and Isidor Straus, who eventually moved to New York after the Civil War and founded a huge retail empire that included Macy's.

Although no documents exist to prove a direct link, Zion Episcopal is reminiscent of the designs of renowned architect Richard Upjohn, author of the 1852 book *Upjohn's Rural Architecture,* who supplied plans for a number of parishes in that era. The church's interior roof support beams are thought to be made of rare white cedar from Talbot County forests. Massive beams, all connected by wooden pegs and mortise-and-tenon joints, support the bell tower.

Some pins were handmade by a local blacksmith's shop. Candle sconces were originally attached to each balcony support beam, and the outline of those sconces is still visible today. A single oil lamp that was attached to one of the support beams was lowered and raised in the center of the sanctuary.

The key to the massive front doors is six inches long, and the original 1848 lock still works. The gallery is also unaltered. Before the Civil War, it provided the designated seating area for enslaved people who were encouraged to attend but were not permitted to sit in the main sanctuary.

A $305,000 renovation project was completed in 2021. In 2023, additional money was raised to restore the historic 1850 Pilcher organ. The church has been listed with the National Register of Historic Places since 1974.

A church history noted that native walnut was used to create the altar, communion rail, lectern, and prayer desk. Rising behind this scene are two medieval-style, crenelated parapets—a reminder of the Gothic design theme seen in the exterior. These parapets enclose two small chancel rooms.

The organ located in the gallery is the oldest hand-pumped organ made by famous organ maker Henry Pilcher and Sons in the United States. It was installed in 1850—and it still works.

Light floods in through the high, Gothic, lancet windows. Original closed, walnut pews with pointed, trefoil ends sit on wide floorboards. Octagonal flared-top, wooden columns support the gallery above and its Gothic-style balcony enclosures.

This elevated section above the main sanctuary was referred to as the "slave gallery" in the years before the Civil War. Enslaved persons were encouraged to attend services with their enslavers but were required to sit separately in this gallery. In more recent years, this space has been used for the choir.

PHOTOGRAPHY BY SCOTT FARRAR

Sharon Methodist

TALIAFERRO COUNTY ORG. 1886

According to a church history written in 1972 by Christine Davidson Brown, Sharon Methodist Church was an offshoot of Raytown Methodist Church, also located in Taliaferro County. The Sharon church was organized on September 24, 1886, with thirty-eight members, many of whom transferred their membership from Raytown Methodist.

On November 1, 1890, its trustees paid $700 for 4 acres of land approximately two miles from the Raytown church and built a meetinghouse that would serve the congregation for twelve years. Then, under the leadership of Benjamin Graham and William Pressley Lovejoy, a new church was erected around the turn of the century.

A Mr. Norton of Crawfordville was reportedly the contractor for the new church, and the congregation made its final payment for building costs on November 2, 1903. The new church was built in the Queen Anne style, made popular around the period 1875–1900 but rarely used in rural churches. Some of the characteristics of this style were asymmetrical facades, decorative wood trim, cross gables, and towers or turrets.

Close by, in the little crossroads town of Sharon, are two other historic churches. Locust Grove Catholic, organized in 1792, is the oldest Catholic church in Georgia. Its present building dates from 1884. South Liberty Presbyterian was organized in 1820. Its present building was constructed in 1877.

A close look at the details of the church construction reveals many of the Queen Anne features, the most obvious being the large turret incorporated into the main entry. The asymmetrical entry and the ventilated turret with offset windows are very unusual, as is the decorative entryway that includes eight small columns.

The main entrance on the left opens onto a large and well-lighted alcove, opposite a small room under the smaller exterior turret. The four rectangular windows with transoms provide light for the sanctuary. The church's interior also features a suspended chandelier and matching casing and wainscoting.

The sanctuary is highlighted by an arched ceiling. In keeping with the exterior architecture, the altar and the recessed apse are asymmetrically flanked. The choir loft is recessed on one side of the pulpit and receives light from two exterior windows. Note the exterior access to the loft.

The view from the pulpit to the front features in-line suspended chandeliers and the customized pews arranged to accommodate the classic double-aisle flow pattern. The soft blue walls contrast with the white framing and wainscoting.

Of the 362 documented interments in the cemetery, thirty-nine carry the surname Kendrick. The obelisk in the foreground marks the graves of John Roberson Kendrick (1846–1926) and his wife, Lizzie Brown Kendrick (1849–1910). John's Confederate pension application states he served with the First Georgia Volunteers under the command of General Marcellus Stovall. Although the application does not give the date of his enlistment, Kendrick would have been fifteen years old at the beginning of the war and eighteen when he was wounded in the siege of Atlanta on August 25, 1864. His application states he had a serious head wound above his left eye and part of his right index finger shot off. After the war he fathered five children and lived till the age of eighty.

PHOTOGRAPHY BY STEVE ROBINSON

Red Hill AME

TERRELL COUNTY ORG. 1890

Red Hill African Methodist Episcopal, also known as Turner Chapel AME, is located on a dirt road in a remote part of Terrell County, with no signs of habitation for miles. Its cemetery is unkempt and covered with weeds. It is another example of the "Almost Gone but Not Forgotten" category of churches that populate the Georgia backcountry. Based on some of the oldest interments in the cemetery, we estimate the congregation was formed in the early 1890s.

The old cemeteries often yield interesting stories that tell us a lot about our history, and a good example is the story of the Flewellen family. The patriarch of the family was Jacob Samuel Flewellen (1845–1915). His headstone is made of specialty marble and gives the impression of a higher level of prosperity than you would expect, given the simplicity of the abandoned church. In addition, we find that Jacob was born into slavery in 1845, which means at the end of the Civil War, he would have been twenty years old. His first wife, Mattie, who died in 1895, was almost certainly born a slave as well.

For most of his life, according to census records, Jacob could neither read nor write. However, the census of 1910 reported that he had become literate. Records also reveal that over the course of his life he purchased land, borrowed money, and paid a poll tax to vote. Clearly, he and his family had enough wealth for an expensive gravestone.

Flewellen is an unusual name, and we suspect Jacob took it from his former enslaver following emancipation—a common practice. There were several slaveholders in the area named Flewellen. Of them, James T. Flewellen enslaved the largest number of people—seventy-six. Born in Jones County, Georgia, in 1828, he attended Oxford

College and the College of William and Mary and graduated from Harvard Law School. He was both a lawyer and a plantation owner. During the Civil War, he was a lieutenant colonel in the Thirty-Ninth Alabama Infantry Regiment.

Once abandoned, these old structures deteriorate rapidly. Eventually, the roof becomes compromised and the death spiral begins. Soon, there will be nothing but the cemetery to remind us of the important events that took place here.

Here is a close-up view of the abandoned organ. That the church owned not only a piano but an expensive organ like this one signifies the congregation was relatively well-off at some point.

Here lies Jacob Samuel Flewellen (1845–1915). Though he was born into slavery and could neither read nor write for much of his life, he acquired property in the years after emancipation and was relatively prosperous. Records show that in 1893, he signed a promissory note for a buggy harness. On April 12, 1898, he purchased just over 200 acres from W. J. T. Whaley for $1,400.

Mattie Marshall Flewellen was the first wife of Jacob Samuel Flewellen. She almost certainly would have been born enslaved, although we do not know a birth date. She died in 1895. His second wife was Lucy Harper Flewellen (1877–1932). Two of Samuel's daughters are buried in the family plot as well.

PHOTOGRAPHY BY STEVE ROBINSON

Bethany Congregational

THOMAS COUNTY ORG. 1891

Bethany Congregational Church is one of two Congregational churches in the Deep South that Ambassador Andrew Young pastored in the 1950s. The other is Evergreen Congregational, located in Beachton, a small community about twenty miles away. Both are on the National Register of Historic Places. (For more information about Ambassador Young's service to these churches and their influence on him, see the foreword.)

Bethany Congregational was established in 1891 to serve boarding students at Allen Normal and Industrial School, as well as day students and their families. The school was sponsored by the American Missionary Association, an arm of the United Church of Christ interested in providing education for Black southerners after the Civil War. The school was initially founded in Quitman, Georgia, in 1885, in a building donated by Mrs. F. L. Allen of Connecticut. But only six weeks after it opened, white arsonists burned down the building. The following year the school relocated to a one-story frame building in Thomasville, and then to a new school ground provided by Judge Hopkins, the mayor of Thomasville.

Although the school closed nearly a century ago, Bethany continues to serve the community of Thomasville. The National Register of Historic Places refers to it as "a small, vernacular wood-framed church with a Latin-cross plan and simple Gothic detailing." The original building, constructed in 1891, "was a rectangular structure supported on brick piers with a steeply pitched roof and a small entrance portico on the front (north) facade." The church was renovated and enlarged in 1914. The National Register concludes that the cross arm of the current church was probably the original structure.

AFRICAN AMERICAN HERITAGE HYMNAL

This photo highlights the Gothic detailing of the windows and pews, along with the paneled tongue-and-groove ceiling. The number and placement of the windows provide abundant light.

The Gothic elements of the pews and upper windows are unlike any we have seen in other rural churches. The opaque lower sash provides abundant but diffused light.

Upon entering the sanctuary, you can see that the raised chancel and apse are the focal point for the church. Musical instruments are on the right, and the traditional piano is on the left.

The 1914 architect did a superb job of creating space for the thriving congregation while preserving the 1891 historical elements.

The interior of the church has two small rooms on the left and right, which were original to the 1891 structure. The tongue-and-groove wainscoting provides symmetry with the rectangular paneled ceiling.

PHOTOGRAPHY BY STEVE ROBINSON

Springhill Methodist

THOMAS COUNTY ORG. 1823

Springhill Methodist is the oldest church in Thomas County. Although it has not held regular services since the 1970s, county residents and church trustees intervened to save the building from complete destruction, and a total restoration was completed in 2011.

Often, the history of a church this old is hard to come by. We are fortunate to have a good written history that was prepared by John Ferrell in 1924. Here is an excerpt.

> This church was organized under a bush arbor during the summer of 1822 [or] 1823 by Peter McKinnon, Lockland Morrison, Angus Morrison and one other pioneer whose name is lost. . . . This chapel was called Spring Hill because of the many natural springs coming out of the high hills of the surrounding countryside. For many years the people who came here to worship drank from the cool spring below the church.
>
> Within a decade the log church was too small to accommodate the growing congregation in a growing community. The new church at the present site was built in 1833. . . . In the 1830's and 1840's it was the banner church of South Georgia and Middle Florida, its membership being about 500. During the early 1820's and 1830's quarterly meetings were camp meetings comparable to the present homecomings except longer than one day. . . . Services were held at 11:00 in the morning and again at night. Conversions ran into the hundreds. . . .
>
> Thus, we see the fleeting history of a grand old mother church which fostered all the churches in this countryside for forty years. Spring Hill was then in the Florida conference. After the Civil War, the old church could not hold the lead anymore, but such shouting, singing, and preaching as was once heard in these hallowed walls has no equal anywhere except at Pisgah in Leon County, in the early 1830's and 1840's.

We are grateful to Mr. Ferrell and to the citizens of Thomas County for their preservation efforts.

Thanks to a restoration and preservation program completed in 2011, Springhill Church sits on its original foundation looking virtually as it did almost two hundred years ago.

From the foundation to the floors, walls, ceiling, roof, and furnishings, the church trustees ensured a faithful renovation.

This view from the pulpit accentuates the simplicity of the sanctuary. The 4-inch-wide heart pine floors support handmade pews with double-plank backboards. These pews may look uncomfortable to today's parishioner, but they were a vast improvement over the footed, half-log, backless benches they replaced.

120
Rock of Ages, Cleft for Me
Savior, Like a Shepherd Lead Us
121
THE GOSPEL OF JESUS CHRIST
REPENTANCE AND FORGIVENESS

Music was a significant element in rural churches. It was an activity in which all could participate and that brought the congregation together. The earliest convenient music-making instrument, after the personal fiddles and guitars of congregants, was the piano.

This black-and white photo captures the spirit of the Springhill legacy. We have seen many renovations but none that are more authentic—a wonderful piece of Georgia history is now perfectly preserved for generations to come.

The inscription reads, "This tomb was erected to the memory of Isabella Morrison—consort of Angus Morrison—Who died in the triumphs of a gospel faith June the 9th 1843 aged 30 years—Leaving a husband, children, numerous relatives to mourn the loss of an affectionate companion, a fond dutiful mother, and faithful friend who always made it her motto in life to live the life of the righteous that her latter end might be as his."

J. W. and Amanda Carroll had five children born between 1882 and 1893. Only one of them lived to be an adult. Here are the four graves of the Carroll siblings—all died before the age of three.

PHOTOGRAPHY BY SCOTT FARRAR

Williams Creek Baptist

WARREN COUNTY ORG. 1787

Williams Creek is one of the oldest Baptist congregations in Georgia. It was constituted December 22, 1787, as the Baptist Church of Christ at Williams Creek. Willis Perry gave the land on which the church was originally built, just northwest of the present site, on the headwaters of Williams Creek. However, this spot proved to be less than ideal since, during heavy rains, the creek would overflow and flood the cemetery and the land surrounding the church. At some point in the latter part of the nineteenth century, the church was moved to its present location on higher ground.

The current building sits on an unpaved road in a remote part of Warren County, created in 1793 from parts of Burke, Columbia, Washington, and Wilkes Counties. The architecture is Greek Revival, standard for many of the early churches in this part of Georgia. The adjoining graveyard holds the remains of several Revolutionary War veterans who settled this part of Georgia shortly after the Treaty of Augusta ceded the land between the Ogeechee and Oconee Rivers to the new state of Georgia in 1783. In the woods nearby is a spring-fed, outdoor baptismal pool.

According to Robert Gardner's *History of the Georgia Baptist Association, 1784–1984*, a split occurred in the church in the early 1820s. One faction followed Billington Sanders, who left Williams Creek to become the first president of Mercer Institute in 1833. The other group, which was larger, followed Thomas Rhodes, who had preceded Sanders as pastor. In 1822 the minority faction petitioned the Georgia Baptist Association (GBA), bringing charges against Rhodes of a serious nature "affecting his moral character."

In an unusual action, the GBA responded with a resolution stating, "The members of Williams Creek, who have connected themselves with said Rhodes, be therefore declared no church, but a disorderly faction. Further that the part of Williams Creek Church who have remained unmoved by the said Rhodes, are hereby declared the proper church, and their conduct has the unqualified approbation of this body." Rhodes was excommunicated in 1822 but later restored to full membership.

Little has changed in the old church except for the electric fans and lights suspended from the original bead-and-board ceiling. The podium rests on a simple raised chancel. The back wall was added some years ago to create storage space, so the present sanctuary is somewhat shorter than the original.

The six-over-six sashed windows allow abundant light into the sanctuary, illuminating the handmade pews and floors made from Georgia heart pine.

From the chancel, the view is of a simple country church with a central aisle and double doors leading to the porch and into the yard. The pews, floors, and high bead-and-board ceiling appear to be original. The four-column Greek Revival architecture was common for the period.

The acoustics in this church are perfect for a piano like this one. Many Baptist hymns, so vital to the faith, have been played here in this remote rural location.

On a wooded hillside in the lee of the church is a deep, spring-fed baptismal pool. The ritual of total immersion is integral to Baptist theology, and baptisms were held in nearby streams or rivers, or in manmade pools like this one.

Mrs. Emily Mosley Thompson was born May 21, 1806, and died October 23, 1890, at the age of eighty-four. According to the 1850 Warren County census, her husband, Jeremiah, was employed as a blacksmith. The grave on the left is that of her grandson, John Belle Thompson, who died in 1884, and the grave on the right is that of his sister, Maggie Belle Thompson, who died in 1880. Both died before their second birthday.

PHOTOGRAPHY BY SCOTT FARRAR

Antioch Baptist

WASHINGTON COUNTY ORG. 1834

Antioch Baptist, constituted on January 17, 1834, is situated on Stephen's Creek on land donated by David Curry and William May. It was founded by elders Jessie Moon and Guthridge Ivey with ten charter members, some of whom came from Bethlehem Baptist Church.

The church served white and Black congregants until 1868, when the Black members withdrew to establish what would become Holly Springs Baptist Church. In January 1885, Antioch reported fifty-three male and ninety-nine female members. This sort of gender disparity was common all over the South in the aftermath of the Civil War, since so many white males between the ages of eighteen and thirty-five had died in the conflict.

The church is located on a dirt road, miles from the nearest homes and businesses. Like so many other rural churches, it lost its congregation many years ago. And though it looks plain from the outside, the interior and the old cemetery give the place a quiet dignity.

The sanctuary is a perfectly preserved, nineteenth-century rural church—a step back in time, when the church was the center of everything for these early Georgia settlers. All rural life, social contact, governance, and spiritual sustenance came from the church. The original founders and many of their descendants are buried in the cemetery in a field of broomstraw.

This photo, taken several years ago, shows the deserted sanctuary of Antioch Baptist. Although some letters are missing, the message on the wall is still legible: "Glory to God in the Highest."

The church is on a red dirt road in a remote location. Some minimal maintenance has been performed to stabilize the structure, and most of the windows are boarded with plywood.

Time has taken its toll on the old piano in the corner, but it is not hard to imagine the sounds of the traditional Baptist hymns that have been sung here since 1834.

The view from the pulpit reveals the simple construction techniques of an early nineteenth-century rural church and the durability of the longleaf Georgia pine that served as the main construction material. The rusty tin roof still keeps the sanctuary dry.

ANTIC

This double headstone memorializes Marguerite Currie Walker and her daughter, Marguerite Hattie. The elder Marguerite died March 4, 1873, three days after her daughter's birth. Little Hattie lived only sixteen days and died March 17, 1873. Note the outhouse in the background.

Scattered in the broomstraw field behind the church are 101 headstones. Thirty-five carry the surnames Curry and May, the original land donors for the church. There are almost certainly unmarked graves there as well.

PHOTOGRAPHY BY SCOTT FARRAR

Phillips Mill Baptist

WILKES COUNTY ORG. 1785

Phillips Mill is one of the most prominent and historic Baptist churches in Wilkes County. It is named after the gristmill belonging to Joel Phillips where, according to the church minutes, sixteen people met in 1785 and agreed to start a church. The principal organizer was Silas Mercer, the father of well-known Baptist leader Jesse Mercer, whom the church ordained just a few years later, in 1789.

Upon Silas's death in 1796, Jesse succeeded him as pastor and served in that capacity for the next thirty-seven years. Jesse also became a significant benefactor and leader of Mercer Institute (later Mercer University), a Baptist school originally located in Penfield that was named in his honor. After the Civil War, in 1871, the Georgia Baptist Convention voted to move the university to Macon, Georgia.

The original location of the church was on the Phillips Mill property donated in 1785. However, in 1848 the church authorized the purchase of the Salem Presbyterian Church building and property, located approximately four miles away. The purchase price was $350. The minutes reveal quite a number of improvements were made to the church building, and it served the congregation well until the church you see here was built in 1907.

Phillips Mill's cemetery records are somewhat confusing, which is not unusual. There are a few older marked graves under Presbyterian ownership (prior to 1848), but only four headstones from 1848 to 1900, when the church was under Baptist ownership. Given the number of church members and normal attrition, there should be far more graves than this. However, as we have frequently discovered, the old cemeteries usually bring more questions than answers.

We think the primary reasons for this historical confusion are the lack of good recordkeeping, certainly, and also the presence of so many unmarked graves. Slowly, the old graveyards will begin to reveal more answers with the aid of today's mapping technology and digital sharing of information. Meanwhile, we have many old burial grounds remaining to remind us of Georgia's history and the people who made it.

The History of Wilkes County by Robert Marion Willingham tells us that in December 1905 a building committee was appointed by Phillips Mill Church, and a legacy donation of $107 from Jesse Asbury formed the seed money for that building program. At the dedication on May 12, 1907, Rev. D. W. Key presented the sermon, and a Mr. Griffin gave a historical sketch of the church, stating that "Phillips Mill had been transformed into an airy, resplendent temple compared to other nearby, rural churches of the time."

The soaring stained-glass windows on each wall, atypical for a remote rural church, allow warm light to spread throughout the sanctuary.

The wooden coffered ceiling treatment was popular in the late Victorian era and is found in many churches built in the 1900s. This photo also shows the organ in the gallery.

Here lie Silas (1745–96) and Dorcas (1746–1819) Mercer. Both were originally buried on the family farm, close to what is now Ficklen, about seven miles away. On October 12, 1976, they were reinterred here at Phillips Mill, the church that Silas helped to found and that their son, Jesse, served as pastor for thirty-seven years. Silas died at the age of fifty-one. Some sources report the cause of death was a mule kick to the head.

Since immersion is fundamental to the Baptist faith, congregations often constructed their churches near creeks or rivers, or they built spring-fed baptismal pools like this one. Judging from its location, we believe that this pool was likely connected to the 1848 church, and while it clearly underwent some renovations over the years, it has been out of use for some time.

In 1785, Revolutionary War veteran Joel Phillips (1727–92) donated land for the church at the site of his gristmill on the Little River, about four miles from the church's current location. We surmise that his remains lie in an unmarked grave near that site. Since Phillips Mill Baptist has been at its current location since 1848, the marker pictured here is likely a cenotaph in his honor.

Selected Bibliography

BOOKS

Alexander, Adele. *Free Women of Color in Rural Georgia*. Fayetteville: University of Arkansas Press, 1991.

Allen, Jane Hack, Virginia Fraser Evans, and Liberty County (Georgia) Board of Commissioners. *Liberty County, Georgia: A Pictorial History*. [Hinesville, Ga.?]: Liberty County Board of Commissioners, 1979.

Amor, E. H. *The Cemeteries of Greene County, Georgia*. Athens, Ga.: Agee Publishers, 1987.

Asbury, Francis. *Journal of Rev. Francis Asbury: Bishop of the Methodist Episcopal Church*. 3 vols. New York: Lane & Scott, 1852. Accessed at http://books.google.com.

Banner-Herald. History in Word and Picture of the Progressive Primitive Baptists. Thomasville, Ga.: Birdwood College, 1955.

Bell, Malcolm, Jr. *Major Butler's Legacy: Five Generations of a Slaveholding Family*. Athens: University of Georgia Press, 1987.

Bonner, John C. *A History of Georgia Agriculture: 1732–1860*. Athens: University of Georgia Press, 1964.

Boykin, Samuel. *History of the Baptist Denomination in Georgia*. Vols. 1–2. Paris, Ark.: Baptist Standard Bearer, 1881.

Bryant, Jonathan M. *How Curious a Land: Conflict and Change in Greene County, Georgia, 1850–1885*. Chapel Hill: University of North Carolina Press, 1996.

Carter, Jeff. *Ancestors of Jimmy and Rosalynn Carter*. Jefferson, N.C.: McFarland & Co., 2012.

Clark, Erskine. *Dwelling Place: A Plantation Epic*. New Haven, Conn.: Yale University Press, 2005.

Cole, Mildred Jackson, and Mt. Enon Historical Committee. *From Stage Coaches to Train Whistles: History of Gum Pond, Mt. Enon, Baconton in Mitchell County, Georgia; 1856–1976; Including Biographical Sketches and Genealogies of Pioneer Families*. Baconton, Ga.: Mt. Enon Historical Committee, 1977.

Crowley, John G. *Primitive Baptists of the Wiregrass South: 1815 to the Present*. Gainesville: University Press of Florida, 2013.

Dickerson, Dennis. *The African Methodist Episcopal Church: A History*. Cambridge, U.K.: Cambridge University Press, 2020.

Erskine, Noel. *Black Theology and Black Faith*. Grand Rapids, Mich.: Erdman's Publishing Company, 2023.

Erskine, Noel. *Plantation Church: How African American Religion Was Born in Caribbean Society*. New York: Oxford University Press, 2014.

Gardner, Robert G. *A History of the Georgia Baptist Association, 1784–1984*. Atlanta: Georgia Baptist Historical Society, 1988.

Gourley, Bruce Thomas. *Baptists in Middle Georgia during the Civil War*. Macon, Ga.: Mercer University Press, 2011.

Harden, William. *A History of Savannah and South Georgia*. Vol. 2. Chicago: Lewis Publishing Co., 1913. Accessed at http://files.usgwarchives.net/ga/chatham/bios/gbs527flannery.txt.

Hemperley, Marion R. *Historic Indian Trails of Georgia*. Athens: Garden Club of Georgia, 1989.

Henderson, Lillian, ed. *Roster of the Confederate Soldiers of Georgia, 1861–1865*. Vol. 4. Hapeville, Ga.: Longino and Porter, 1960.

History of the Baptist Denomination in Georgia. Atlanta: Jas. P. Harrison & Co., 1881.

History of the South Georgia Conference: The United Methodist Church, 1866–1984: With Historical Sketches of the 713 Active Churches. [St. Simons Island, Ga.?]: South Georgia Conference Commission on Archives and History for the Bicentennial of American Methodism, 1984.

History of Warren County. Warrenton, Ga.: Warren County Chamber of Commerce, n.d.

Inscoe, John C. *The Civil War in Georgia: A New Georgia Encyclopedia Companion*. Athens: University of Georgia Press, 2011.

Johnston, Richard M. *Dukesborough Tales: The Chronicles of Mr. Bill Williams*. Upper Saddle Creek, N.J.: Gregg Press, 1968.

Jones, Ethelene, Dale Dyer, Blue Ridge Kiwanis Club, and Fannin County High School GAMA. *Facets of Fannin: A History of Fannin County, Georgia*. Dallas: Curtis Media Corp., 1989.

Jones, George Wimberly. *Observations on Dr. Stevens's History of Georgia*. London: Forgotten Books, 2013 [1849].

Jordan, Robert H. *There Was a Land: A History of Talbot County, Georgia*. Talbotton, Ga.: [Robert H. Jordan?], 1971.

Keister, Douglas. *Stories in Stone: A Field Guide to Cemetery Symbolism and Iconography*. Layton, Utah: Gibbs Smith, 2004.

Kilde, Jeanne Halgren. *When Church Became Theatre: The Transformation of Evangelical Architecture and Worship in Nineteenth-Century America*. New York: Oxford University Press, 2002.

Kilpatrick, W. L. *The Hephzibah Baptist Association Centennial*. Augusta, Ga.: Richards and Shaver, 1894.

Knight, Lucian. *Georgia's Landmarks, Memorials, and Legends*. Elmwood, La.: Pelican Publishing Company, 2006.

Krakow, Kenneth. *Georgia Place-Names*. Macon, Ga.: Winship Press, 1975.

Leslie, Kent Anderson. *Woman of Color, Daughter of Privilege: Amanda America Dickson, 1849–1893*. Athens: University of Georgia Press, 1996.

Mallary, Charles. *Memoirs of Elder Jesse Mercer*. 1844. Reprint, London: Forgotten Books, 2018.

McWhirter, Cameron. *Red Summer: The Summer of 1919 and the Awakening of Black America*. New York: Henry Holt, 2011.

Meyer, Richard, ed. *Cemeteries and Gravemarkers: Voices of American Culture*. Logan: Utah State University Press, 1992.

Morgan, Phillip. *African American Life in the Georgia Lowcountry*. Athens: University of Georgia Press, 2011.

Morton, William J. *The Story of Georgia's Boundaries: A Meeting of History and Geography*. Atlanta: Georgia History Press, 2009.

Pierce, Alfred. *A History of Methodism in Georgia*. Atlanta: North Georgia Conference Historical Society, 1956.

Raper, Arthur F. *Tenants of the Almighty*. London: Macmillan, 1943.

Raper, Arthur Franklin, and Ira De Augustine Reid. *Sharecroppers All*. Chapel Hill: University of North Carolina Press, 1941.

Raper, Arthur Franklin, and Martha J. Raper. *Two Years to Remember and Other Writings*. Vienna, Va.: Jean Moore, 1977.

Rice, Thaddeus Brockett, and Carolyn White Williams. *History of Greene County Georgia, 1786–1886*. Macon, Ga.: J. W. Burke Company, 1961.

Robinson, R. L. *History of the Georgia Baptist Association*. [Atlanta?]: N.p., 1928.

Rozier, John. *The Houses of Hancock, 1785–1865*. Decatur, Ga.: Auldfarran Books, 1999.

Schley County Preservation Society and Mrs. H. J. Williams. *History of Schley County, Georgia*. Roswell, Ga.: W. H. Wolfe Associates, 1982.

Shepard, Jacquelyn M. *Cemeteries and Churches of Quitman County, Georgia*. Self-published, [1988?].

Smith, Doris Gunn, and Ways Baptist Church. *Ways Baptist Church, Stellaville, Georgia, Jefferson County: Minutes 1817–1900; History 1817–1917*. Evans, Ga.: Doris Gunn Smith, 2003.

Smith, George G. *The Story of Georgia and the Georgia People*. Macon, Ga.: George G. Smith Publishers, 1900.

Smith, George Gillman. *The History of Methodism in Georgia and Florida: From 1785 to 1865*. Macon, Ga.: J. W. Burke & Co., 1877.

Southern Historical Association. *Memoirs of Georgia: Containing Historical Accounts of the State's Civil, Military, Industrial, and Professional Interests and Personal Sketches of Many of Its People*. Vol. 2. Atlanta: Southern Historical Association, 1895.

Stevens, William Bacon. *A History of Georgia*. New York: D. Appleton & Co., 1847.

Sullivan, Buddy. *Early Days on the Georgia Tidewater*. Darien, Ga.: McIntosh County Board of Commissioners, 1995.

Upjohn, Richard. *Upjohn's Rural Architecture: Designs, Working Drawings, and Specifications for a Wooden Church, and Other Rural Structures*. New York: Da Capo Press, 1975.

Wetherington, Mark V. *The New South Comes to Wiregrass Georgia, 1860–1910*. Knoxville: University of Tennessee Press, 1994.

Williams, David S. *From Mounds to Megachurches: Georgia's Religious Heritage*. Athens: University of Georgia Press, 2008.

Willingham, Robert Marion. *The History of Wilkes County, Georgia*. [Washington, Ga.?]: Wilkes Publishing Co., 2002.

ARCHIVES IN GEORGIA

Georgia Baptist Church Records, Georgia Baptist History Repository, Special Collections, Jack Tarver Library, Mercer University, Macon. https://mercer.libguides.com/ld.php?content_id=53357185.

Georgia Baptist Convention Historical Archive and Museum, Atlanta.

UMC North Georgia Conference Archives, Pitts Theology Library, Emory University, Atlanta.

UMC South Georgia Conference Archives, Arthur J. Moore Methodist Museum and Library, St. Simons Island.

PAMPHLETS, PRINT ARTICLES, AND WEB

"About Lumpkin Campmeeting." Lumpkin Campmeeting. Lumpkincampmeeting.org/about.

American Yawp. Stanford University Press Edition. Americanyawp.com.

Ancestry. https://www.ancestry.com/.

Augusta Chronicle. https://augustachronicle.newsbank.com/.

Bethany Congregational Church nomination form. National Register of Historic Places. 1985. https://catalog.archives.gov/id/93209605.

Birdsville Plantation nomination form. National Register of Historic Places. 1971. https://catalog.archives.gov/id/93208736.

Brown, Christine Davidson. "History of the Sharon Methodist Church, Sharon, Georgia." 1972. Special Collections and Archives, Pitts Theology Library, Emory University. https://s3-us-west-2.amazonaws.com/pittsarchives/mss028/pdf/SharonSharon4.pdf.

Brown's Guide to Georgia. Peachtree City, Georgia. www.brownsguides.com.

"Camp-Meeting Grounds." *New Georgia Encyclopedia*. November 20, 2013. www.georgiaencyclopedia.org/articles/arts-culture/camp-meeting-grounds.

"The Church of Jesus Christ of Latter-day Saints in Georgia." Wikipedia. Last edited July 3, 2024. https://en.wikipedia.org/wiki/The_Church_of_Jesus_Christ_of_Latter-day_Saints_in_Georgia.

"Coastal Bryan Heritage Trail: Rice Cultivation on the Ogeechee River." Richmond Hill Historical Society. http://www.richmondhillhistoricalsociety.com/history-driving-trail.html.

Cooksey, Elizabeth B. "St. Marys." *New Georgia Encyclopedia*. September 24, 2014. www.georgiaencyclopedia.org/articles/counties-cities-neighborhoods/st-marys.

"Cumorah Church." Satilla River Saints Project. https://www.satillariversaints.org/cumorah.

Davis, Randall. "Historic Rural Churches of Georgia: There Is No Law in Georgia for Mormons." *Georgia Backroads* 17, no. 2 (Summer 2018): 23–27.

Digital Library of Georgia. https://dlg.usg.edu/.

Encyclopedia Virginia. https://encyclopediavirginia.org/.

FamilySearch. https://www.familysearch.org/en/united-states/.

Ferrell, John. "Spring Hill Methodist Church History." 1924. Thomas County, Georgia, Archives—Church Records, USGenWeb Archives. http://files.usgwarchives.net/ga/thomas/churches/springhi143bb.txt.

Find a Grave. https://www.findagrave.com/.

"Findings and Recommendations Conference on Education and Race Relations." *Broadcaster: The Official Journal of the Tennessee State Association of Teachers in Colored Schools* 6, no. 1 (1933): 14.

Friends of Cemeteries of Middle Georgia. http://friendsofcems.org/.

GALILEO. www.galileo.usg.edu/?Welcome.

Georgia Historic Newspapers. https://gahistoricnewspapers.galileo.usg.edu/.

Georgia Historical Society. http://www.georgiahistory.com/.

Georgia Trust for Historic Preservation. www.georgiatrust.org.

Google Earth. https://earth.google.com.

"The Great Migration (1910–1970)." National Archives. Last reviewed June 28, 2021. https://www.archives.gov/research/african-americans/migrations/great-migration.

Hacker, J. D. "From '20. and Odd' to 10 Million: The Growth of the Slave Population in the United States." *Slavery & Abolition* 41, no. 4 (2020): 840–55. https://doi.org/10.1080/0144039X.2020.1755502.

"Historical Atlases and Maps of U.S. and States." Maps of US. www.mapofus.org/.

"Historical Maps." Hargrett Rare Book and Manuscript Library, University of Georgia, Athens. https://www.libs.uga.edu/darchive/hargrett/maps/colamer.html.

"Historic Buildings: Nichols-Hunnicutt-Hardman House and Farm." Sautee Nacoochee Center. www.snca.org/snc/museums/history/homes/bldgHardman.php.

"Historic Presbyterian Church in Georgia Kept in a State of Preserved Decay." Forgotten South. https://theforgottensouth.com/mt-zion-church-hancock-georgia/.

"History of the Methodist Church, Jewell, Georgia." 1950, revised 1981. Special Collections and Archives, Pitts Theology Library, Emory University. https://s3-us-west-2.amazonaws.com/pittsarchives/mss028/pdf/RockMills.pdf.

"History of White Oak." White Oak Associate Reformed Presbyterian Church. https://www.whiteoakarp.org/history-of-white-oak.

"Index of /ga/banks/military/civilwar." USGW Archives. http://files.usgwarchives.net/ga/banks/military/civilwar/.

"Indian Springs State Park History." Georgia Department of Natural Resources, State Parks & Historic Sites. https://gastateparks.org/IndianSprings.

Jones, Mary Callaway. *Mercer at Penfield: 1833–1871: Centennial Celebration*. 2nd ed. May 27, 1933. 20 pp. https://ursa.mercer.edu/handle/10898/2851.

Kilpatrick, W. L. *The Hephzibah Baptist Association Centennial, from 1794 to 1894*. http://baptisthistoryhomepage.com/ga.hephzibah.assoc.hist.html.

McClure, Greg. *History of Ridgeway Baptist Church*. Georgia Baptist Church Records, Georgia Baptist History Repository, Special Collections, Jack Tarver Library, Mercer University, Macon.

McCollum, Louise. "Bethel Presbyterian Small, but Is History." *Chattanooga Press*, October 5, 2005.

McWhiter, Cameron. "The Spiritual Ground of History." *Harvard Divinity Bulletin* 39, nos. 3–4 (Summer/Autumn 2011). https://bulletin.hds.harvard.edu/the-spiritual-ground-of-history/.

"The Namesake Chapel." *Cumorah Junction* (blog). April 4, 2012. https://cumorahjunction.blogspot.com/.

National Register of Historic Places. National Park Service, U.S. Department of the Interior. https://www.nps.gov/subjects/nationalregister/index.htm.

Needwood Baptist Church and School registration form. National Register of Historic Places. 1998. https://catalog.archives.gov/id/93208438.

New Georgia Encyclopedia. University of Georgia Press and Georgia Humanities Council. www.georgiaencyclopedia.org/.

Old Stone Church nomination form. National Register of Historic Places. 1979. https://catalog.archives.gov/id/93207259.
"Our History." Academy Baptist Church. https://www.academybaptistchurch.com/about.
"Our History." St. Andrew's Episcopal Church. https://standrewsdarien.org/history/.
"Possum Trot Church." Berry College. https://berry.edu/about/our-rich-history/possum-trot-church.
QPublic. https://qpublic.schneidercorp.com/.
Ramsey, Clayton H. "Historic Rural Churches: Grooverville Methodist." *Georgia Backroads* 16, no. 1 (Summer 2017): 23–26.
RootsWeb. https://rootsweb.com/.
Slave Voyages Consortium. Slavevoyages.org.
St. Bartholomew's Church nomination form. National Register of Historic Places. 1982. https://catalog.archives.gov/id/93207355.
"Taliaferro County History—Taliaferro County Historical Society." USGenWeb Archives. http://files.usgwarchives.net/ga/taliaferro/history/tchsfiles.txt.
Tate, Brittany. "Deaconess Alexander's Influence Still Permeates throughout Isles." *Brunswick News*, October 31, 2015. https://thebrunswicknews.com/life/deaconess-alexanders-influence-still-permeates-throughout-isles/article_f3c50d6b-5139-5d97-a03f-0bac855e9e60.html.
Virtual Vault. Georgia Archives, University System of Georgia. https://vault.georgiaarchives.org/.
Wikipedia. www.wikipedia.org/.
Wood, Betty. "Slavery in Colonial Georgia." *New Georgia Encyclopedia*. Last modified July 27, 2021. https://www.georgiaencyclopedia.org/articles/history-archaeology/slavery-in-colonial-georgia/.
Zion Episcopal Church nomination form. National Register of Historic Places. 1974. https://catalog.archives.gov/id/93209562.

About the Photographers

In addition to being talented photographers, these volunteers are passionate advocates for the rural churches and skilled researchers who are a vital part of the process. Many times the history for the old churches is available only in obscure places and local sources. Much of the discovery, research, and documentation is done in the field by this dedicated group.

TONY CANTRELL

Photographs of Indian Springs Baptist and Corinth Methodist

I'm an Air Force brat, living in Georgia since 1977. I got into photography with my job selling government surplus, and it kind of blossomed from there. I've always loved traveling the back roads to see all the gorgeous little towns in Georgia. When you dig a little deeper, you see that they all have a story to tell, with the church usually being the starting point. I try to capture that in photographs and preserve the history.

RANDY CLEGG

Photographs of Rockwell Universalist, Bethel Presbyterian, Ruckersville Methodist, and Mount Airy Presbyterian

An amateur photographer from Buford, Georgia, I began to learn the craft and to be intentional with the photos I take after purchasing my first digital SLR camera in 2007. To learn photography I studied beautiful photos, and those on the Historic Rural Churches of Georgia (HRCGA) website made me want to contribute to these efforts.

RANDALL DAVIS

Photographs of Bethlehem Primitive Baptist, Union Methodist, Fair Haven Methodist, and Walker Grove Baptist

A freelance photographer now residing in Statesboro, Georgia, I took up photography after working as a land surveyor and cabinet and furniture maker and completing a tour as a platoon leader in the army. I also worked as a research biologist in fisheries for the Alaska Department of Fish and Game. My interest in history and preservation of significant structures brought me to HRCGA, especially the documentation aspect of their goals.

SCOTT FARRAR

Photographs of Siloam Presbyterian, Mount Zion Presbyterian, Rock Mills Methodist, Union Primitive Baptist, Zion Episcopal, Sharon Methodist, Williams Creek Baptist, Antioch Baptist, and Phillips Mill Baptist

I am a hobbyist photographer, born and raised in Georgia, currently residing in Atlanta. My love of history was sparked while attending the University of Georgia, and I have spent many years since exploring and photographing much of rural Georgia. I've been fortunate enough to be associated with HRCGA since the beginning, and it has given me the opportunity to combine my love for Georgia history and my photography.

CYNTHIA JENNINGS

Photographs of Cumorah Church of Latter-day Saints

I was born in Kentucky, but I consider Spartanburg, South Carolina, my hometown. I am an educator by day, but I spend much time taking road trips to find old cemeteries and buildings and researching their history. I am always in search of lesser-documented places. I get great joy in sharing what I find online via social media or on my website, To Die for Images (todieforimages.com).

JOHN KIRKLAND

Photographs of Ways Grove Baptist and Bethel Brick Methodist

I am a photographer living in Augusta, Georgia, on the banks of the Savannah River. Photography for me started out as a necessity to capture memories of my children, but it has become a passion—maybe even an obsession. Since here in Augusta we are surrounded by many old towns, churches, and architecture, all set in the charm of the classic South, much of my photography focuses on the historical.

WAYNE MOORE

Photographs of Bryan Neck Presbyterian, St. Bartholomew's Episcopal, Needwood Baptist, Walthourville Presbyterian, and Wayfair Primitive Baptist

An early interest in photography led me to pursue a bachelor's degree in photography from the Savannah College of Art and Design. My company, Back River Photography, allows me to live out my passion of photographing the Low Country and its people. The history and architecture—particularly of old churches—of Georgia's coastal region inspire me.

SAM RATCLIFFE

Photographs of Possum Trot Church

I am a native of Oakman, Georgia, in Gordon County, currently living in Rome. After I earned BA and MBA degrees from Rome's Berry College, my career included operations management, human resources, and training. I have been an amateur photographer for over fifty years after receiving my first 35 mm camera in college. My favorite subjects are people and travel photography.

TOM REED

Photographs of Mount Carmel Methodist, Old Stone Church, Lumpkin Campground, Tarpley Chapel, Chubb Chapel Methodist, Ridgeway Baptist, and Academy Baptist

I graduated from the Southeast Center for Photographic Studies in Daytona Beach, Florida, back in the days of film and wet darkrooms. I worked at a variety of photography jobs, and I also was a freelance photographer for NASCAR, covering major stock car races. I then retired after twenty-five years as chief photographer at the *Gainesville Times*. Since retiring I have been able to spend my time working on photography that I enjoy, rather than what is assigned to me, mainly landscapes and travel photography.

STEVE ROBINSON

Photographs of Grooverville Methodist, Hopewell Missionary Baptist, Phillippi Primitive Baptist, Providence Methodist, Friendship Baptist, Red Hill AME, Bethany Congregational, and Springhill Methodist

From Leesburg, Georgia, I am a husband, father, grandfather, and amateur photographer. For years I have enjoyed exploring and photographing the rural areas of south Georgia. Small country churches have always been a vital part of the rural Georgia landscape and were once the center of life for the communities they anchored. I attempt to document their simple beauty to help tell their stories.

GAIL DES JARDIN SEGARS

Photographs of White Oak Presbyterian, Glendale Chapel Methodist, and Odessadale Methodist

In 1992, I was neck-deep in listening to R.E.M. and following the interests of lead singer Michael Stipe, whose photography hobby piqued my interest. As a child, we lived next to the only cemetery in town, and I grew up fascinated by its character and mystery. This fascination with churches and cemeteries has stayed with me, and photography has become a natural avenue for paying reverence to these spiritual gathering places.

CATE SHORT

Photographs of Swords Methodist

I was born and raised in Athens, and an appreciation of Georgia's rural landscape was instilled within me at a young age as my grandparents introduced me to the areas where they spent their own childhoods. We would often pick up a disposable film camera on our way out of town, and I've since spent countless hours photographing historic structures and cemeteries. I'm honored that I've been able to dedicate some of that time to assisting in the documentation, and subsequent preservation, of Georgia's historic rural churches.

BRYAN STOVALL

Photographs of Mizpah Methodist, Good Shepherd Episcopal, St. Andrew's Episcopal, and Walker Grove Baptist

Deeply rooted in Georgia, my passion for photography began in my childhood hometown of Martin, in the state's northeast. Finding inspiration from friends at the University of Georgia, I honed my artistic skills and embarked on a successful photography career. After two decades capturing images of families and weddings, I shifted focus to the captivating beauty of Savannah, its architecture and history, and the surrounding landscapes. Now my lens documents the natural world and historical treasures, supporting causes close to my heart.